UNDER FURRED HATS
(6th A.L.H. Regt.)

Brig.-General C. F. Cox, C.B., C.M.G., D.S.O., V.D., First Commanding Officer 6th A.L.H. Regiment.

Under Furred Hats

(6th A.L.H. Regt.)

BY

GEO. L. BERRIE (Lieut.)

The Naval & Military Press Ltd

Published by
The Naval & Military Press Ltd
5 Riverside, Brambleside, Bellbrook
Industrial Estate, Uckfield, East Sussex,
TN22 1QQ England
Tel: +44 (0) 1825 749494
Fax: +44 (0) 1825 765701
www.naval-military-press.com
www.military-genealogy.com
www.militarymaproom.com

DEDICATED TO
OUR FALLEN COMRADES

FOREWORD

IN the following pages I have briefly described during its term of service abroad, the career of the 6th Light Horse Regiment, from December, 1914, to August, 1919.

Written in 1919 from memory, aided only by the scanty information to be gleaned from the Regimental War Diaries, the narrative is unavoidably incomplete in many respects, and I can only ask the indulgence of my readers in this regard.

At this late date it has also been very difficult to obtain a really complete series of photographs, and my thanks are due to members of the Regiment, notably Lt.-Col. Fuller, Major Tooth, and Corporal Marsh for the use of their collections.

I have attempted in the narrative and accompanying sketches to portray that spirit and morale which were unshakeable features of the Regiment's career, and if the perusal of this little book brings back memories of the good—the work accomplished no matter how hard or dangerous, in those days of glorious mateship—and helps forgetfulness of the bad—the petty annoyances and heartburnings—then this souvenir of its service is more than justified.

THE AUTHOR.

DECORATIONS AWARDED THE REGIMENT

D.S.O. AND ORDER OF THE NILE
Lt.-Col. C. D. Fuller

D.S.O.

Major H. D. White, Major S. A. Tooth, T.-Major H. S. Ryrie

M.C.

Lt. R. G. Black, Lt. H. Dickson, Lt. R. B. Ronald, Capt. H. Hardy, Capt.-Chaplain A. H. Teece

D.C.M.

Sergt. P. Ryan, Lieut. W. T. Macansh, Lieut. F. L Ridgway, Sergt. J. M. Bargh, Sergt.-Major B. P. Sheridan, Cpl. C. H. Livingstone

M.M.

Lieut. C. R. Capel, Sergt. D. Baird, Sergt. H. Thompson, Sergt. R. J. Foster, Tpr. W. Bassett, Sergt. W. Potter, Sergt. T. Sheridan, Sergt. S. G. McNair, Cpl. D. Smith, Sergt. McNamee, Cpl. Hindmarsh, L.-Cpl. F. Arnott, Sergt.-Major W. Kilpatrick

CROIX DE GUERRE
Major M. F. Bruxner

SERVIAN STAR
Hon. Capt. J. Hanton

MEDAILLE MILITAIRE
Q.-M. Sergt. J. Cheater, Sergt. H. Foran

CONTENTS

ILLUSTRATIONS

CHAPTER I

THE BIRTH AND TRAINING OF THE SIXTH

ALL roads led to Victoria Barracks. From city, village, farm and farthest-out station they came during the dying months of 1914; a never-ending stream of men borne thither by the variable tide of their own reasons.

Who could in those early days analyze or fathom his own reasons? The "old soldier" came back. There was the man who sensed change, excitement and travel; the gambler who decided on the spin of a coin; and there was he who felt instinctively that man's greatest job was at hand. There came the man who saw all his mates going and the many thousands who could find no reason at all save the irresistible magnet of a great unknown adventure.

Blended into the early Australian Battalions and Regiments, they formed a true volunteer army; they acquired a corporate pride and belief in themselves that is difficult of attainment save amongst men who enrol together, train and drill together, and finally start off scratch to test that training and themselves. Such was the material of which the 6th Light Horse Regiment was formed in September, 1914.

It is not too much to say that during its early training days; those days at Rosebery Park, Rosehill, Liverpool and Holdsworthy, the 6th Regiment acquired one of its most valuable assets, that quiet confidence in itself which characterized it as a unit throughout, and which time and time again justified its possession.   From the enrolling stage at Rosebery Park, and throughout its various Australian camps, the Regiment trained steadily. Both men and horses were carefully selected; finally, on December 19th, 1914, Lieut.-Col. C. F. Cox marched his Regiment out of Holdsworthy for embarkation, and early next morning the *Suevic,* with the Regiment on board, moved from its berth at Woolloomooloo and dropped anchor out in the harbour.   Early in the afternoon the *Suevic* cleared Sydney Heads and the first stage of the Regiment's active service commenced.

Taken as a whole the voyage was uneventful. Few horses were lost; the health and spirits of the unit were excellent; and one and all looked forward eagerly to their first sojourn, in uniform, on foreign soil.

After brief stays at Aden, Suez, Ismailia and Port Said, the voyage of the *Suevic* finally came to an end on the 1st of February, 1915, at Alexandria.

Disembarking the same day, the Regiment entrained to Cairo, and, walking and leading horses, proceeded to Maadi, where it took over part of the camp previously occupied by the 1st Light Horse Brigade.

By the 7th of February, various details from other transports marched in and the personnel of the Regiment was practically complete.

Camped on the edge of one of Cairo's few white

Regimental Lines, Maadi, February, 1915.

B

At the head of C Squadron Lines, Maadi, 1915. Designed by Sergeant S. McNair.

spots, the Regiment settled down to the task of completing its training, exploring between-whiles the mysteries of an ancient Eastern City.   The English residents of Maadi worked nobly for the comfort of all ranks; recreation huts, a soldiers' club and tobacco store, were speedily provided, and many an early Light Horseman in Egypt will ever remember gratefully .the genuine hospitality of English homes open to them without any differentiation as to rank.

Beyond the camp lay the training grounds; a few miles of sandy waste bounded by the Mokattam Hills.   We got to know those hills pretty thoroughly; we reconnoitred them, captured them at the extended gallop, and did outpost against an imaginary foe.   We despatched foraging expeditions which generally returned with nothing but an alarming thirst; we built stone walls and dug trenches, we drove each other from hill to hill and finally fought a pitched battle with the 1st Brigade out towards the "Petrified Forest." Needless to say both Brigades claimed a victory. We spent days on the rifle range, we route marched to Helouan and the Barrage; we took the new and enthusiastic soldier's pride in our horses and gear; and all the while the rumour of something big afoot whispered incessantly in our ears.

The Infantry were going somewhere, that was certain; and where was there a handy battleground where we and our horses would be of any use? We began to look askance at our steeds; were they to be our albatrosses?   Finally we knew that the

Infantry had gone somewhere; slowly news came
to us magnified and distorted of the "Landing,"
but as we were destined to know a few weeks later,
the wildest figment of fiction that leaked through
to us paled beside the reality.   Then we knew that
the Infantry were only hanging on, and an insistent longing permeated the Regiment to be allowed
to volunteer to go to their aid.   Rumours came and
went that we were going, and finally, the climax
came one night at the Stadium, where General
Ryrie announced to the Brigade the news of our
early departure for Gallipoli.

Much has been written of the vehement eager-
ness of the Light Horse Regiments to take part in
the Gallipoli undertaking.   But some had to be
detailed to stay behind with the horses, and many
a man after vain endeavours to be included in
the marching out strength, quietly marched out
independently and turned up out of the stokehold
when the transport was well at sea.   Beyond an
issue of infantry ruck-sacks and puttees, the Regiment retained its Light Horse equipment; a short
route march or two and the preparation was over.

The Transition

"To the halt, on the left form platoon."
The old mess huts at Maadi rang with strangely
unfamiliar shouts, the while a Lance-Jack, with a
smattering of infantry drill, tried vainly to initiate
his section into the art of forming fours.
"Cut it out, Corp.," remarked a burly bushman
from his perch on the table.   "I'll bet you all you

Swimming Horses at the Delta Barrage, May, 1915.

won at the two-up school last night that we never leave the horses."

"You haven't got the latest, though," returned the Lance-Jack, "the storeman belongin' to the R.Q.M.S. says he saw indents go in for new equipment a few days ago and there was one for Tommy rooksacks, and the Orderly-room Sergeant says the 1st Brigade is going for a cert. in a few days."

"Well, why don't they send us," another chipped in; they want us bad enough, and for all the good the horses will ever be to us they might as well give the lot to the Gyppos. The blasted war will be over before we get a smell."

"I wonder who'll be left behind if we do go," speculated a third.

"Why 25 per cent. and all farriers and transport drivers."

"Here's one transport driver who won't be left in Maadi, anyway," chimed in a tall fair-haired lad from Albury.

"You're just the one who will be left, Snow," came a chorus of replies. "Old Robby doesn't love you well enough to take you over there to get potted."

"Well, we can see some stoush at the Stadium, to-night, even if we can't get the real thing. Bonsoll, the middleweight Tommy, is fighting Cameron out of the 2nd Regiment, and there'll be mobs over out of the 1st Brigade. The "Old Brig." is refereeing and there's oceans of booze in the canteen; it ought to be some night."

Slowly the crowd dispersed to the tent lines. Only the usual afternoon stables cut into the ceaseless quest for dinkum "furphies," and the speculation concerning, and elaboration of the latest and most startling. Signallers went about with an exasperating air of possessing secret information, and the orderly trooper reposing in the shade of the tent, never listened more acutely to the snatches of telephone conversation or the confabs between the Adjutant and the C.O.

But the arrival in the evening of big batches of men from the 1st Brigade, and the early rush to the Stadium in anticipation of the evening's boxing, eclipsed temporarily the one insistent thought uppermost in everyone's mind. The Stadium was packed to its uttermost capacity. Practically the whole Brigade, and, in addition, the visitors from the 1st Brigade and the Tommy Garrison from the prison camp, were seated round the ring.

Several preliminary bouts over, the event of the evening—Bonsoll, an ex middleweight champion of Ireland, and Cameron, a lean, tough-looking Queenslander—was announced. A ten-round contest, brimful of incident, game and clever, ended in the Brigadier's decision being given to Bonsoll on points. The excited plaudits of the Tommy contingent over their representative's win, were seconded no less heartily by the vast concourse of Light Horsemen present.

Thoroughly worked up by the evening's sport, on top of the intense anxiety as to the longed-for move, breathless silence cut instantaneously through the vociferous cheering as General Ryrie walked into the centre of the ring and held up his hand. Instinctively every man in the vast gathering knew what was coming, and the very air seemed charged with the welter of mental emotions in every breast, now pent up to breaking point

As if to emphasize the supreme drama of the moment, the "Old Brig." remained with uplifted hand for several moments before he began.

"Lads," and his powerful voice carried to the furthest corners of the Stadium, "this is the first chance I've had of addressing you since our mates fixed bayonets in earnest over yonder, and I want you to join me in three cheers for our gallant comrades in the Infantry, the men who made the world ring with their deeds on the 25th of April, and who are now hanging on and in dire need of help. Now then"—and the vast volume of cheering echoed and re-echoed over the desert spaces and the quiet streets of Maadi.

"I know that you are all anxious to give them all the help you can, and I can tell you to-night on the best authority that it won't be many days before we are alongside of them."

Then a veritable pandemonium of sound broke loose. Hundred of hats flung repeatedly sky-wards; hundreds of men wringing each other's hands; a babel of cheering, yelling; a tumultuous surging backwards and forwards of the excited throng; the floodgates of human emotion had burst

at last, and the intense anxiety of the past ten
days, mingled with the haunting fear that the
chance would not come had at last been allayed.
They had the "Brig's." word for it; they were
going.

CHAPTER II

EARLY DAYS ON GALLIPOLI

MAY the 14th, 1915, will always dwell in the memory of the early members of the Regiment. After dark that evening, the parade quietly assembled, and except for a general tenseness of feeling and the burden of the rucksacks, it might have been an ordinary night route march. But from Bab-el-Louk to Cairo station, the feelings of the Regiment found vent in a vociferous answer to the cheers of the population. And many a broken section was completed before the Cairo platform was reached. Infantrymen, wounded lightly at the landing, and anxious to return, quietly fell in as we marched along. Eagerly we plied them with questions and as eagerly drank in their answers. And with one and all the main reason for going back was—their mates. Entering, as we were, the threshold of one of the great moments of life, a moment of intangible and fascinating mystery, the sight of these infantrymen, and the knowledge of what their action stood for, quickened in us the blood of manhood already stirred by the prospect of the great unknown.

The night passed, a welter of physical and mental emotions; the march through Cairo, the crowded troop train, and finally, at daybreak the transports lying alongside the wharf at Alexandria. We embarked during the morning on the *Lutzow*, a name which stood for a long time as an example of what a troop transport should *not* be. But packed as we were, and suffering the worst of accommodation and sanitary arrangements, who cared? At the most it was for a few days, and everyone was in the humour to make allowances. We sailed from Alexandria on the afternoon of the 15th of May, and on the morning of the 18th, passing by Cape Helles, beheld the truly thrilling spectacle, as it was then, of a naval bombardment and an aeroplane surrounded by puffs of smoke.

Finally, on the evening of the 19th, after a run along the edge of the war zone, we anchored off Anzac Cove, and spent a large part of the night listening to incessant rifle fire. We had come to a war at last. All night long the heavy firing continued, waning only with daylight, and by mid-day arrangements had been made for our disembarkation. In broad daylight we took our places on lighters and mine sweepers, and headed towards Anzac Cove. Each vessel as it drew in to the beach ran its gauntlet of shrapnel; cover on board was indifferent, the shooting was excellent, and the curiosity of many extreme. But our landing was effected and our first baptism of fire cost nothing in casualties.

We neared the landing-places; the rugged cliffs and scrubby hills frowning down on the narrow patch of shingle, brought to us in full force the almost incredible feat the infantry had performed.

a few weeks previously, and as we struggled up Shrapnel Gully through thick low scrub, and along single file pads, the general feeling of wonderment became intensified. We reached a point where a friendly pinnacle hid us temporarily from view, and here we received orders to dig in.

As if to emphasize the order a number of shells fell in quick succession unpleasantly close to our camping area. In remarkably quick time every man had a funkhole of some sort handy, and practised the rabbit act many a time during the afternoon. But for the evidence of the grim reality on every side of us, the picture of Shrapnel Gully that spring afternoon would remain indelibly impressed on many a memory.

Gradually widening from the Neck, as its slopes approached the beach, the valley, emphasized at intervals by abrupt knolls and sharp gulleys, lay clad in the soft green of the holly and arbutus, speckled at intervals by a species of everlasting. And the setting sun cast the shadows of Imbros and Samo-Thrace like a gentle pall, over what became later, the graveyard of many of our best, the ultramarine of the placid Aegean Sea.

The Regiment's casualty list was inaugurated early. Trooper Berghelin, of C Squadron, received a shrapnel pellet in the eye soon after landing, and Colonel Cox, on the following day, was wounded in the leg and evacuated.

The big engagement of the 19th of May produced its aftermath of night activity. The Turkish trenches vomited a constant and rapid fire

from dark until daylight, and till the evening of
the 22nd the Regiment stood to in Shrapnel Gully
in nightly expectation of a repetition of the Turkish attack.

We discovered early what "fatigues" meant on
Gallipoli.   Road-making, water-carrying, ration-
loading, wood-gathering—we were fresh and
eager; but our anxiety was mostly directed towards
knowing when and where our turn in the trenches
was coming.   About mid-day on the 22nd, we
moved in single file up a track made slippery by
rain, towards the Neck.   Branching off to the right
into a deep sap, we wound along a narrow and
tortuous communication trench.   The occasional
crack of rifle fire sounded directly overhead.   At
length we took possession of our sector of the
front line, relieving part of the First Infantry
Brigade.   Our range card showed Lone Pine about
half right, Johnson's Jolly to the front, German
Officers' trench and the Chessboard to the left.

Initiated into the use of a periscope few will
forget that first glimpse of No Man's Land and
the Turkish trenches. Just in front of our sector
lay one of the few flat pieces of ground on the
whole line; to right and left it broke into gullies
heading towards Lone Pine and the unoccupied
marine trenches.   The gullies were piled with
Turkish dead, and the flat ground from almost our
own parapet to that of the enemy was dotted with
inanimate forms, and as if in pity the wild
everlasting swayed gently in the spring breeze.
The costly defeat sustained by the Turkish

Army a few days previously, had resulted in feverish digging activity by day, and rapid firing by night.

We settled down quickly to the routine of trench life. Dug as it was in action, our sector needed a good deal of consolidation and improvement. So for the 28 days we remained in possession, continuous work, in addition to observation post duties, prevailed; sapping, tunneling, beach fatigues and road-making.

NIGHT POST

"Any scran left, Sergeant?"

The Bushman leant his rifle against the wall of the communication trench, and put the question with an air more hopeful than expectant.

"Your section drew it; spoonful of spuds and a drop of Joe Smart's onion tea. You're back late, aint you?"

"I stopped half-an-hour at the corner well trying to get a drink. Had to come away then without a mouthful."

"Better get your tea into you then, you're on post to-night. Number one post and second shift."

"What about possies?"

"Some of them are camping on the firestep and some in the sap; there's only the green stripe possy empty."

"Hell," muttered the Bushman.

He picked up his rifle, pushed past the tunnel fatigue carrying bags of earth to the dump in the rear, and made his way to where Number One Post

c

was stationed. Silently he located the drop of tea
and mushy vegetable mixture, and groped about
for a tin of bully and a biscuit. Sitting on the firestep he had just about completed his meal, when
the sergeant on shift appeared and moved over to
where several huddled figures lay on the firestep.
"Your shift," he whispered, touching one. The
figure sat up, yawned, rubbed his eyes, and seized a
rifle leaning against the side of the bay. The Bushman picked up his and followed him to the Observation Possy, where a motionless figure stood
gazing through a loophole. Silently the relief took
place.

The Bushman took his stand, with fixed bayonet,
in the bottom of the trench, his mate clambered up
alongside the observer and took over the loophole.
For half-an-hour he remained there. Fifty yards
away lay the Turkish trenches. A succession of
rifle shots came at regular intervals. Mostly
aimed too high they whistled harmlessly over the
parados, but an occasional "phut" on the sand-bags
round the loophole made the observer wonder
were they only flukes or was the place marked.
Only last night . . . It seemed hard to be potted
like a rabbit looking out of a burrow. Surely on a
night like this they couldn't locate a loophole at
the distance, unless a sniper had crawled out.
Something moved, or was it a flicker of light, a
rat, or a swaying of the low scrub. Wasn't the
half-hour up? "Bill!" The Bushman climbed up
beside him. "Just on the tick, old son. See anything?" "I can't be sure," came the whispered

reply, "but they keep peppering the loophole and I could swear I saw something move near that dead Jacko straight in front.   I saw a flash twice that seemed closer than their trenches.   Don't look over, Bill"

A second later the Bushman's head was lowered.

"Nothing moving just then, anyway.   Damn these loopholes," he thought savagely, "you can see nothing through them except things that don't exist.   Another few shifts on nights of this sort and that boy will be done; he's as good as gone now."

His usual custom was to chance a look over the top every five minutes if the firing wasn't too heavy.

The night was cloudy and windy.   Through the loophole the utmost eye-strain could tell him nothing, but the fitful starlight enabled the Bushman to reassure himself in a momentary glance over the top.

A movement of the grass, the gleam of light on a tin, a darker patch of shadow and the shapeless blotches of humanity, anything or nothing at all would put the wind up a man, once his nerve began to go.   And he wouldn't get the wind up. Better risk a bullet through the head than lose his confident alertness and break up like the boy standing in the trench below him.   Stay, something *did* move then, near the dead Jacko.   Perhaps the boy was right.   Stopped now, but there was no glint of light there before.   He *must* chance a look over.

A jet of flame and a breath of air on his cheek.
Some clods rolled off the parados on to the boy
below.   Like a flash he was alongside the Bushman, leaning against the bay wall and breathing
hard.

"Bill, did he get you?"

"No; but close enough.   You were right, lad;
there's a sniper near the dead Jacko, and he's ours.
I'm going round into the next bay.   I can get a
good shot there between the sandbags.   When I
chuck a clod over put your hat up over the parapet."

A few seconds later the clod fell and up went
the hat.   Two almost simultaneous reports, a
bullet hole in the hat and then quiet.

"We'll know in the morning if we've got him,"
whispered the Bushman.   Our shift's finished, the
sergeant's waking that chap on the firestep.   You
turn into his nap."

A minute later the Bushman stumbled along the
firing line and turning down a sap stopped in front
of a long and narrow hole scalloped in the wall.
From the loose earth piled above a stripe of
greenish moisture oozed out, and trickled to the
floor of the sap.   Someone—no one knew whom—
had been buried there in the days of the landing,
by the natural formation of the sap.   Crawling
into the narrow cave, the Bushman, feverishly
anxious to make the most of his two hours, closed
his eyes and endeavoured to forget the narrow
escape of his just finished shift.   But sleep refused to come.   He might as well have kept on

shift and let some other poor devil have the rest.
That stink overhead was awful. He could almost
hear the ooze dripping.   Something fell on him.
What odds.   If those cursed tunnellers were only
carrying their dirt along any other sap, he might—

"Wake up, Bill; your shift. Gosh! the blow-
flies must be bad where you come from. You're
lyin' in a nest of squashed maggots!"

   * * * * * *

An eight-hour armistice had been arranged for
the 24th of May.   It came none too soon.
Towards eight o'clock in the morning, the
hour fixed for the cessation of hostilities, firing
died away on either side, and a white flag, followed
by a red crescent and a party of Turkish stretcher-
bearers, appeared on the enemy parapet.   Simultaneously our own burial parties went over the top.
An approximate boundary line was pegged in No
Man's Land, and the grim task of collecting and
interring the dead began.   A large number
had to be buried where they lay, others on
our side of the boundary were rolled into stretchers,
carried over and delivered to the Turkish burial
parties. Prominent officers on either side stood at
the boundary and interchanged such ideas as they
could. The occupants of the trenches were under
strict orders to keep well under cover, but the
curiosity regarding one of the most remarkable proceedings of the campaign, found vent in many a
hurried glance between sandbag gaps, and snap-
shots taken of the world at large through loop-

holes. A few of our own men, mostly on our own side of the line, were recovered and identified, but the day's work was for the Turkish Army, and the dead buried along the whole front ran into many thousands, an eloquent reply to their boasted intention of driving the Australian into the sea. By four in the afternoon the work was completed, the burial parties were withdrawn, and the armistice, strictly observed by both sides, came to an end in a brisk interchange of rifle fire.

On the 19th of June, with a strength of 16 officers and 403 other ranks, the Regiment left the trenches for a spell. Twenty-eight days in the line had resulted in a considerable casualty list, but sickness had not yet begun to raise its head to any extent. That was reserved till later. We moved round to Deadman's—later known as Rest—Gully, and established ourselves there, hoping for a well-earned rest before being asked to take up another front line sector. The hope was as short-lived as the rest. That same Saturday evening the digging of Chatham's Post began. Loading up at dark with pick and shovel, 220 rounds of ammunition, rifle, rations and waterbottle, the Regiment moved up hill and across valley towards the extreme right of the Anzac position. There we emerged into No Man's Land, close to the water's edge; a long sap was pegged out, and, covered by a party some distance in front, we dug. The phrase "swinging it," and the spirit which it embodied, was unknown. All night long picks and shovels rang unceasingly; just before daylight we collected our gear and an exhausted body of men stumbled, gasping, over the hills towards Rest Gully, and climbed with dragging steps to the possies on the terraces above.

The weather had now become' intensely hot. Few men there were who were not on day fatigues; and continuous night digging completing the sap and forming the first redoubt on Chatham's Post, broke, to all intents and purposes, the health of the Regiment. Dysentery and diarrhœa made their dread appearance, and at the end of ten days, when we moved to our position in the Brigade sector, on the extreme right, the iron grip of disease was indelibly stamped on the personnel of the Regiment. Among the casualties to date, the deaths included Sgt. Parkes, and Troopers Murray, Brown, Jefferey, Bonnar, Pattrick, Bellinger and Dunn; and the wounded, Captain Bruxner, Lieut. Hordern, Sgts. Moffat, Collins, Pattrick, Lamborne, and Cpl. Baldie.

DIGGING CHATHAM'S

Rest Gully! at sundown.

Not too much rest about it, it seemed to the Bushman as he sat in his possy on the top terrace. They had come out of the trenches early that morning and the fatigues shifting Headquarter's stuff round from the top of Shrapnel Gully had been solid and lasted well up to mid-day. He was feeling none too good; a touch of dysentery had sent him on sick parade that afternoon and the M.O. had put him off duty. Everyone had hoped for a few days real loaf, and here was the whole Regiment falling in on the roadway across the gully for an all-night digging stunt.

One of the senior Majors was talking and fragments of what he was saying drifted across: "Dangerous job."   "Likely to be under fire." "New position on the right flank."   "Infantry won't tackle it."   "We'll show 'em," etc., etc. All the usual guff.

The Bushman got up and put a few things into his haversack. He threw on his gear, and descending to the roadway, quietly fell in on the end of the line. The sunset glow was fast dying away as the party moved in single file up over the first ridge and commenced the descent into Victoria Gully. Rifle and full gear, with an additional 60 rounds, haversack, waterbottle and either a pick or a shovel made the Bushman hope that the new position wasn't too far away.

The pace was slow—it had to be—and fully an hour passed before the long line filed across Shell Green and down a steep narrow sap towards the beach. Then, through a brief tunnel, it emerged out into No Man's Land, a fairly flat strip with a steep ridge rising on one side and the wavelets of the Aegean Sea lapping on the other. The ground had been already pegged out. Several hundred yards of communication sap seemed to be the first job, and with little delay each man was placed on his allotted ground. Pick and shovel were plied unceasingly. The earth, save in very few places, was bad digging; scrub roots and loose stones made shovelling difficult, but silently the long line lowered itself gradually.

The short summer night passed slowly away. Unceasingly men toiled, but the first halt was called as the presage of dawn, the faintest breath of moving air, stirred the stillness of the scrub and stunted pines.   Climbing again the hillside sap, men made their way to Shell Green, stacked their picks and shovels, and moved off in straggling groups for the pad that led over the hills to Rest Gully.

The Bushman realized during his journey back how much of his waning store of vitality the night's work had cost him.   The dead weight around his body and over his shoulders seemed to increase with every hundred yards.   His breath came in short gasps, and the intense weariness of body and soul made him wonder whether he could keep up till he reached his dug-out in Rest Gully.

With sagging steps he began the final climb. Along the winding road, around the dug-outs where exhausted men already lay in the sleep of semi-unconsciousness, up the steps cut in the hillside, and staggering along the top terrace he dropped his gear on one side of the dug-out and himself on the other.

And daybreak came to Rest Gully.

*   *   *   *   *   *

The Brigade took over the extreme right flank of the Anzac position.   The 5th Regiment occupied Chatham's Post, the 6th and 7th taking over successive sectors inland. For some little time we enjoyed the novelty of being a considerable distance from the enemy trenches. From certain concealed spots day observation could be done without a periscope, and by night the hideous strain of loophole observation could be reduced to a minimum. But the approaches from Shell Green to our position were a veritable death-trap. Incessantly "Beachy Bill" paid calls on his way to Anzac Cove, and rarely a day passed without casualties, nearly all in the rear of the front line.

The road to Anzac Beach was partly exposed to snipers from the direction of Gaba Tepe, and fatigue parties had the choice of doubling a few hundred yards along the beach, or climbing a number of heart-breaking hills. Generally they risked it one way. Risks were also cheerfully taken for the sake of a swim at night. The utter absence of fresh water and soap, and the continued occupancy of trenches, had given the louse scourge full play. What wonder the men risked anything from a sniper's bullet to a court martial, for the unutterable relief of a salt water swim. It is difficult to say how much the Aegean Sea contributed towards the upkeep of such health as remained in the Regiment, undermined at it was by continuous work day and night, scanty rations of mostly shocking quality, and unnecessarily primitive sanitary conveniences. The latrine was merely a deep open pit. There the fly pest multiplied in millions and dysentery spread broadcast. Fever and cholera were mostly unknown, due, let us sup-

Shell Green.

pose, to careful inoculation of all ranks. Men who were mere walking skeletons from continued diarrhœa, could be found, if off duty, sleeping nightly alongside a foul latrine pit. Reinforcements were scarce, the small stream coming in was quite insufficient to allow for the evacuation of any save absolute nervous breakdowns.

But the morale of the Regiment remained unchanged. Men endured the depth of physical suffering for the sake of hanging on, of remaining alongside their mates and refusing to be beaten. Early in July the gradual approach of the enemy trenches necessitated the occupation on our part, of Holly Spur, later known as Ryrie's Post. Saps and tunnels were driven across Poppy Valley and gradually linked up; the new line forming the future support trenches of Ryrie's Post. The further digging and consolidation of the position was fraught with considerable danger from snipers, concealed in the almost impenetrable scrub which covered the hollow and succeeding ridge behind Holly Spur. Parties to cover the sappers from surprise attack, lay, day and night, in front of the sapheads. By night snipers fired unceasingly at the sound of the picks and shovels on the ridge above them. Cramped by hours of motionless silence, the covering party, lying in half sections, spent its nights listening alternately to the overhead whistle of lead and the steady working of Mauser bolts less than thirty yards away in the thick scrub below them. By day the slightest movement brought a barrage of shrapnel along the edge of the spur. Lying face downward, or crouching amongst the prickly wild holly, the day post spent its shifts amid torments of heat, thirst and flies. Then, as always, the water supply was very scanty. One pint a day, sometimes not that, was the allowance, beside the meal issue of tea, often so nauseating as to be undrinkable.

On the 12th of July, the digging of Ryrie's Post still being in progress, a demonstration took place along the whole of the Anzac Front with the view of assisting operations then in progress at Cape Helles. Thirty men from C Squadron, under the command of Lieut. Ferguson, advanced across the dip in front of Holly Spur, and taking up a line on the succeeding ridge, opened fire on the Turkish positions in front. Immediately heavy shrapnel enfiladed them from the direction of the Olive Grove; rifle and machine gun fire replied from the Brown trenches, and by the time the withdrawal was ordered, thirteen of the little force had become casualties. Three—Kidman, O'Brien and L/Sgt. Ellis—were killed outright; K. Ronald and Creer died of wounds shortly afterwards, and among the wounded were the brothers Body, the brothers Capel, McCarthy, McKeown, Rodd and Walker. The bodies of O'Brien and Kidman were recovered with great difficulty, costing two more men in the process, Troopers Paul and Wiggins, wounded. For work done on July 12th, Lieut. Ferguson, Sgt. Tooth and Troopers Foster and Fenner were mentioned in despatches.

ONE MAIL-DAY

"Orderly-Sergeant for mail!"

The welcome order was passed eagerly and rapidly along the support trenches and firing line, and the Orderly-Sergeant soon appeared making his way to the main sap leading out to Headquarters, amid a running fire of comment and exhortation.

"Wonder if she's a big one." "Fifty bags on the beach yesterday for the Brigade." "Hope there's some parcels." "Bring me one, Sergeant; I'll do water fatigues for you for a month for just one blooming letter." This from the Bushman seated on the firestep cleaning his rifle. "Poor old Fred," he continued, "hope he gets a good swag of it himself, he hasn't had a single letter since we landed, and it's just about got him down."

The Orderly-Sergeant made his way to Headquarters, and collecting the letters for his Squadron, sat down on the terrace and rapidly ran through the bundle for his own. It was a big mail, scarcely a man in the squadron whose heart would not be gladdened by the distribution; but, for himself, not a solitary letter. And this was the fourth mail since they had landed, and each time he had had to swallow the same disappointment. What *had* happened to his mail. He *knew* they had written and he had written himself every week. It seemed uncanny that his should have been singled out to be sunk, lost, or mislaid. With an effort he tied up the bundle and returned to his squadron in the trenches, nerving himself for the bitter task of handing them out and of seeing the joy in every heart reflected on every countenance. At least his week as Orderly-Sergeant was up that morning and surely some would come before such a task fell to him again.

His appearance in the firing-line was greeted by a roar of expectation. Passing rapidly from hand to hand the letters were distributed and the lucky recipients for a brief space forgot their troubles in their mental flight to home and people.

"No luck, Fred?" queried the Bushman.

The Orderly-Sergeant shook his head and gazed out across the ocean towards Samo-Thrace with a set and bitter look on his face. Then he walked slowly away to his dug-out.

"Well, he's stiff, and no mistake," said a trooper, unfolding a precious missive for the third time. "Stiff enough to get knocked this afternoon. What's the exact strength of the stunt?" to his neighbour in the next bay.

"Only a demonstration. I think," was the reply. "Over the top on to the next ridge and get nicely shelled. There's a big attack on Achi-Baba this afternoon and the idea is we stop reinforcements going down. They're doing the same right along the line."

"More likely to stop a few shrapnel pellets ourselves," grunted the first speaker. "How many going?"

"Thirty, I think. A few out of each troop.

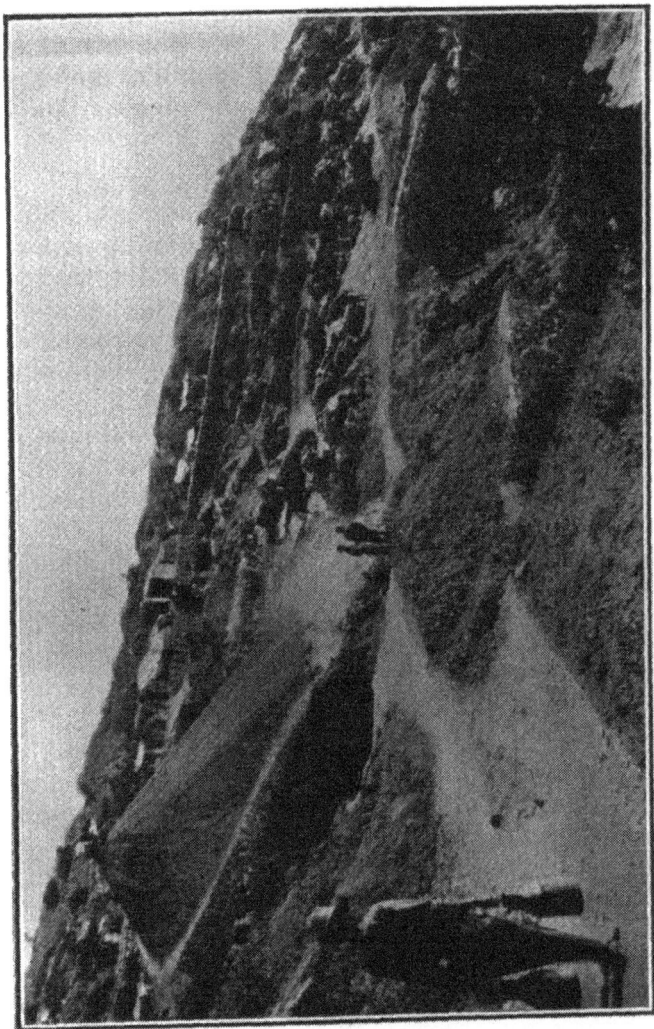

Reserve Areas behind Ryrie's Post.

D

They've not been detailed yet, but I know we're going, and so is Fred. Here goes to give my gun and ammunition a special clean, anyway."

*   *   *   *   *   *

The next spur in front of the trenches was as yet unoccupied. Beyond that again, and across a deep gully the enemy held a strong position, and from it a natural get-away whence reinforcements could easily be hurried towards Cape Helles. Simultaneously with other small bands of "demonstrators" along the Anzac Front, thirty men went over. Moving rapidly through the thick scrub they lay extended on the next spur and with no cover save the semi-invisibility afforded by the prickly holly, poured a rapid rifle fire into the enemy position across the deep gully. But invisibility proved no protection against incessant shrapnel fire. In withering blasts the batteries from the Olive Grove searched for and found the thirty men.

*   *   *   *   *   *

The burial party had been working hard on Shell Green since dusk. But before the first shovelful of earth had been thrown back a figure came running across from Brigade Headquarters.

"Which is Fred's grave?" he panted. "Better put these in with him; they came a few minutes ago in a bag of buckshee mail from the beach," and the shovels rang again over a still figure with a bundle of letters on its breast.

*   *   *   *   *   *

The strength of the Regiment had now been reduced by death, wounds and sickness to 13 officers and 344 other ranks. In a bare three weeks our strength had wasted to the extent of 60 men. A reinforcement of 55 other ranks arrived on the 13th of July; by the end of the month the temporary increase in strength had more than disappeared. The work of trench construction seemed never ending; the heat had now become intense, and the flies unimaginable. To compensate slightly, firing-line activity abated somewhat, as if to prepare for the strenuous month of August, close at hand.

But outside the front line the daily routine continued to be the same ever hazardous undertaking. Never a fatigue left the post without knowing that luck alone would determine whether or not it would be the last. Lieut. Robson was killed by shrapnel on July 24th, and Sgt. Tressilian met his end a few days previously from a sniper's bullet.

Early in August preparations began to be made for a big advance. Kits, blankets and coats were stacked in Poppy Valley, the "white rags" were issued and sewn on, and everyone waited breathlessly for something stupendous to happen. Fortunately, as events turned out, the Regiment was not called on to storm the Turkish positions opposite. The whole episode of Suvla Bay and Lone Pine proved, in the end, ineffectual. Our machine gun section and a squad of bombers took part in the defence of the captured Lone Pine

Entrance to Ryrie's Post.

position and suffered heavy losses, including Lieut. Lang, who died of wounds on the 12th of August.

The casualties among officers necessitated a number of appointments to commissioned rank: R.S.M. Paulin, R.Q.M.S. Thompson, S. M. Jordan, Sgt. Morell, Sgt. Tooth, and Corpl. Close became 2nd Lieutenants.

Towards the end of August, C Squadron of the 12th Regiment, became attached to us as a 4th Squadron, and things settled down again to the drab monotony of trench occupation. Daily the ranks were thinned by sickness and occasional killed and wounded. But by the middle of September a change in the weather took place. Light rain fell and the worst of the summer heat seemed to have passed away.

CHAPTER III

LATER DAYS ON GALLIPOLI

ON the evening of the 16th a demonstration, with heavy shelling, took place along the whole front, the enemy replying briskly with both artillery and rifle fire. A seventy-five struck the top of the parapet at Ryrie's Post, killing Capt. Richardson, Lieut. Buskin and three other ranks. As if in return, the enemy demonstrated vigorously next morning. A bombing raid was attempted on one sector of Ryrie's Post, but was easily and effectively driven back.

For several days demonstration was followed by counter-demonstration. Lieut. Drummond was badly wounded by shrapnel, and Brig.-Gen. Ryrie was also among the casualties, his place in command of the Brigade being taken by Col. Cox, leaving Major J. F. White in charge of the Regiment. On the 2nd of October a welcome draft of reinforcements arrived, Lieut. Hordern and 127 other ranks, bringing the regimental strength (4 squadrons) to 23 officers and 442 other ranks.

October passed by uneventfully; occasional heavy firing demonstrations on either side, and the gradual diminution of sickness being the only noticeable features. Towards the end of the month some bitterly cold days forewarned us of what we might shortly expect, and with the scanty materials available, dugouts were made as weather-proof as possible.   Major J. F. White, who had hung on gamely up to now, was evacuated in a very low condition, and Temp. Major H. D. White took command.

Further promotion to commissioned rank had become necessary, and between September and November the following N.C.O.'s became officers: Sgt.-Major Marks, Sgt. R. G. Black, Sgt. M. C. McKenzie, Sgt. S. M. Menzies, Sgt. H. Hardy, Sgt. N. Dickson, Sgt. A. J. Britten, Cpl. A. Walker, Sgt. K. Alford, Cpl. O. Tooth, Cpl. A. Reynolds, Sgt. R. B. Hedley.

The Regiment's bombing organization had now reached a high state of efficiency.   Enemy rifle and machine gun fire from positions opposite to us were effectively silenced by means of a trench mortar and catapult, the latter worked chiefly by Trooper F. J. Collins, who had since the earliest days made a name for steady courage and un-shakeable nerve.

The gradual advance of the Turkish lines along the spur towards Chatham's Post, made the rear of Ryrie's Post and Poppy Valley very insecure. The 5th Regiment successfully attacked and occupied the most advanced enemy position, and then by sapping and tunnelling, Wilson's Outlook, distant only a few yards from the enemy, was established.   The post became the scene of vigorous bombing duels and a veritable death-trap, but it had the desired effect of preventing any further advance of the enemy towards Chatham's Post.

Major Fuller returned from England on the 20th of November, and a little later took charge of the Regiment vice Lt.-Col. Cox, who assumed command of the 1st Light Horse Brigade. On the 26th inst. the Regiment exchanged places with the 5th Regiment, and took over Chatham's Post and Wilson's Outlook. As if to signalize the change, the weather, which had gradually grown colder, set in wet, with violent windstorms, culminating on the night of the 28th with a heavy fall of snow, the thermometer showing 26 degrees of frost. The trenches were practically unprepared for such weather. Beyond the issue of a few rain coats, we were equipped only for the torrid months just passed by. A few observation posts were roofed with iron, but no sleeping possy was protected by anything but oilsheets. The cold continued to be intense for several days and nights. Numbers were evacuated with frostbitten feet, and the strength of the Regiment became so low that continuous night duty was unavoidable. For 35 consecutive nights one post was occupied by the same three observers. It became second nature to sleep for just as long as the spell lasted, and many an observer offered up a heartfelt prayer when the bright searchlight from our little friend, the destroyer, crept slowly round the beach from Gaba Tepe and rested on the Turkish trenches opposite Wilson's Outlook and the seaward slopes in front of the Beach Post line. The slightest

Lieut.-Col. C. D. Fuller, D.S.O., 3rd Class Order of the Nile, who Commanded the 6th Regiment from November, 1915, until taking Command of the 2nd Light Horse Brigade, December, 1918.

sign of a target on the other side of our red light
glaring seaward was enough to bring a salvo of
shells from the little destroyer's ever-ready guns;
yet, in spite of both guns and searchlight, the
Turks managed to build a barbed wire entangle-
ment right to the water's edge. To our surprise
one morning we saw that about a quarter of the
distance had been completed, and machine guns
and rifles were carefully trained on the spot in
anticipation of the next night's operations. What
it cost the Turks in casualties to complete that line
we could not estimate. As a job we made it as
hot for them as we could; but completed it was
several nights later, and we ungrudgingly took off
our hats to the enemy's courage and tenacity.

In spite of the incessant night duty and intense
cold, conditions had vastly improved. The fly
pest had vanished; lice had abated considerably;
both quantity and quality of rations had improved, and the length of the winter night made
possible at least seven hours sleep, which although
broken, differed very much from the short periods
of the earlier days—-those brief snatches of sleep in
cramped dug-outs, interrupted by false alarms.

During the early part of November we experienced one of the most unique proceedings of
the campaign, known as the "silent stunt." For
a week, along the whole front, not one single
round of ammunition was fired, save for a few
shots from the batteries. The whole position
might have been inhabited by the dead as far as

activity went in the firing-line. As if to make the situation more perplexing to the enemy the silent stunt was followed by several very heavy artillery demonstrations.

On the 10th of December, a number of destroyers, lying well out to sea, off Chatham's Post, bombarded with concerted salvos, Gaba Tepe and the enemy's positions in the neighbourhood of the Olive Grove.

With the abatement of the blizzards of the end of November and early December, came fine and warmer weather, and once more the remaining handful of the Regiment settled down to a philosophic acceptance of trench life, tinctured with speculative wonder as to what would be the outcome of it all. By the middle of the month persistent rumours of an impending move developed into the certainty of a complete and final evacuation. The removal of artillery, the departure of all medically unfit, the destruction of various stores and the different sham fatigues exhibited to the Turkish gaze for mystification purposes, all pointed to the inevitable end. It is difficult to analyze the feelings of the attenuated Gallipoli garrison when the matter was placed beyond all doubt by the issue of evacuation orders.

For those of us who had, throughout seven lurid months, dwelt in an inferno of death and disease, the underlying sentiment was not for ourselves, but for the men who had fallen in a desperate and unsuccessful gamble. The little graveyard at Shell Green, the tiny crosses scattered about Chatham's Post and Poppy Valley, and always the sight of the Aegean Sea, never failed to remind us, if reminder were necessary, of those whom we seemed to be abandoning. But we knew none the less, that the enterprise had failed, and if our hearts were heavy with the thoughts of what Gallipoli stood for, there came eventually the hope of succeeding later in some other venture. And, finally, when parties had to be detailed, competition was keen for a place in the post of honour, the last garrison to leave the trenches.

The dispatch of baggage on the 14th, Cpl. Baird in charge, was the first tangible move made by the Regiment. Numerous shows for the misleading of Turkish observers were instituted. Large parties of men marched solemnly across Shell Green carrying empty water cans and empty boxes into the sap near Brigade Headquarters. A turn to the left and a few hundred yards brought them back to their starting point, and if the Turkish field glasses had been equal to the distance, they would have revealed Brig.-Gen. Ryrie exercising himself with an empty bully beef box on his shoulder. Strangely enough, Shell Green, which had always been a spot particularly favoured by the enemy's shrapnel, was left almost unmolested during the period. So were many points on the ridges behind Chatham's and Ryrie's Posts. It now became apparent that the success of the evacuation depended mainly on the weather, the navy, and secrecy. Silent nights were alternated

with the usual expenditure of rifle and machine
gun fire and bombs. On the 17th heavy weather
appeared to be working up again; slight rain fell
and a stiff breeze prevailed, but on the following
day a lull followed, and everyone wondered if at
least one phase of luck was going to stick to us.
The programme had by now been well mapped
out. On the evening of the 18th the first large
party, 13 officers and 116 other ranks, filed quietly
out of Chatham's Post and embarked safely at
Anzac Beach. The last two days were remarkably quiet along the whole line.

The strength of the Regiment on the last day
consisted of 13 officers and 142 other ranks.
Divided into nine parties they left at various intervals from 6 p.m. to 10.30 p.m., leaving 51 all
ranks to garrison Chatham's Post until the final
move at 2.30 the following morning. The night
was calm and bright moonlight prevailed.
Occasional clouds threw shadows on the trenches
opposite and played tricks with the scrub along the
base of Poppy Valley and the beach.

The destroyer's searchlight swept persistently
the coast line from Gaba Tepe, and occasionally
shot across the hills towards Maidos. The last
parties had been stationed in Wilson's Outlook
since nightfall. Crouched in forward listening
posts they waited, stolidly fatalistic, for the never-
ending hours of suspense to pass. At first a
sniper opposite proved a welcome break, but his
persistence, the regular thud on the parados and

the trickle of dirt soon assumed an iteration that became maddening.

The last night was not a "silent stunt." Shots were fired at intervals from Chatham's Post and the beach line, but Wilson's Outlook remained wrapped in the silent and freezing moonlight. The frozen midnight air chilled thoroughly the small band of watchers during that last long vigil. Neither blankets nor greatcoats were left to possibly hamper their movements. No one closed his eyes even momentarily during those nine lingering hours. Sleep seemed as impossible as the whole proceeding. It seemed incredible that everything should go off successfully; that the enemy should not guess that during those early morning hours all that remained to oppose them was a handful of calmly desperate men.

Just after midnight the faint hum of a distant aeroplane was borne by the night breeze along the thinly-held line. Turkish it proved to be. Passing low along the whole of our line, it seemed impossible that discovery could be avoided. And three shots fired in quick succession by "Beachy Bill" made many a heart steel itself in anticipation of the expected Turkish charge. Was the great forlorn hope to miss after all by a "short head?" It wanted only a couple of hours, at the most, of luck, to bring off successfully the last moments of a desperate gamble. With ears, eyes and souls astrain, the little band remained breathlessly tense for those last gradually fading hours.

Fortune had, though we knew it not, decided in

E

our favour, and one of the great feats of the war
went off without a single hitch.   At half-past one
20 of the remaining 51 filed quietly out; half an
hour later they were followed by sixteen more,
leaving the final party of 2 officers and 13 men in
possession of both positions.   Of these, two men
patrolled the front line of Chatham's Post
glancing occasionally over the parapet towards
Holly Spur, peering into outgoing tunnels, and
meeting every few minutes at the head of the tunnel
to Wilson's Outlook.   The party at the latter post
busied itself setting a number of mechanical rifles
and connecting a number of bombs with slow
fuses.   Timed to go off at intervals for hours after
the departure of the final party, they must have
contributed to the deception of the Turkish
trenches, if such were really necessary.

At last the moment arrived.   Meeting at the
tunnel head at half-past two, the sentries in Chatham's Post heard soft footfalls coming along the
gallery.   Silently they took their places in the line,
and with muffled footsteps the final party of "diehards" followed the long sap up the main ridge
from Chatham's Post, through the top tunnel and
out on the terrace beyond, Lieut.-Col. Fuller
bringing up the rear and blowing out the candles
as he passed.   Pausing a moment at Brigade
Headquarters, where our little band arrived
almost simultaneously with similar bodies from
the 5th and 7th Regiments, we moved across
Shell Green, crossed the head of Clark's Gully,
wound over Gun Ridge, passed through the cover-

ing parties stationed there, and moving by way of
the Beach Sap, reached our rendezvous at "B"
Depot. Few knew the way to "B" Depot better
than the diehards of the right sectors, yet even
that was not left to chance; the road was clearly
marked with a whitish substance. A string of
rowing boats rocked gently alongside the little
jetty. As if in farewell a solitary shell from
"Beachy Bill'—possibly his last—screamed overhead on its flight to Anzac Cove.

With the same silent efficiency that had
characterized the whole of the evacuation, the
boats were rapidly loaded; a steam launch went
ahead and gradually disappeared in the waning
moonlight; we realized that the almost impossible
had happened. As far as our Brigade was concerned not a single mishap had occurred. A mine
sweeper awaited us several miles from the shore.
We climbed out of our row boats, and waited,
shivering and conscious of the inevitable reaction,
for our journey to Lemnos.

By now a series of sheets of flame marked the
coast line from Suvla Bay to North Beach, and a
mighty explosion, the blowing up of Quinn's Post,
followed by an instant crackle of Turkish rifle
fire, had told us that the last man, whoever he was,
had embarked from Anzac. Now that it was all
over there were few who did not feel the unutterable relief. None there were who did not know
that one mistake, one backhand stroke of luck must
have made the concluding hours of Gallipoli the
same story of ghastly tragedy which had lasted

since the landing. For the labour, the suffering and the losses of our blood brothers had been sacrificed, and well we realized it, on the altar of incompetency. But none of the blame attached to the men who fought. And looking back on a never-fading period, the outstanding feature, apart from his courage and dash, was the astounding morale shown by the Australian soldier.

It is almost ludicrous in these later days of experience to look back and remember the needless hardships, the primitive methods and the petty and useless restrictions placed on the trench dwellers. We knew well enough in those days when anyone blundered with regard to the smaller parts of our existence. But the same spirit of pride that made men practically die before they were evacuated, the determination to do a bit better and hang on a bit longer than the next man, lasted right to the bitter end, and it imbued the A.I.F. with the knowledge that its unconquerable belief in itself was justified, as it was right till the firing of the last shot.

In the gradually waning gloom of that Monday morning we moved away towards Lemnos, and a few hours' steam brought us into Mudros Harbour and alongside the troopship *Beltana*. Then we realized the feelings of those who had left us on the previous evenings. Men leant over the deck railing straining their eyes to catch a glimpse of some particular mate; and heartfelt greetings and expressions of relief as our mine sweeper drew up alongside, brought home to us what they had felt;

the men who would have given worlds to have been with us to the last. We quickly transferred to the *Beltana,* and with the exception of a small party on the *Anchises,* the evacuation strength of the Regiment was complete.

For two days we remained in Mudros Harbour, and then the *Beltana* sailed for Alexandria, arriving there early on Christmas morning. That Christmas Day compared well with one in the workhouse. The rations on board throughout had not been remarkable for either quantity or quality. Whether they had been exhausted or not remains one of the mysteries of the war, as far as the humble ranker was concerned at any rate. But Christmas dinner left more spaces unfilled than overloaded, and from three o'clock in the afternoon till nine at night we sat on our kits on the upper deck. Fed only by savoury odours issuing from the saloon we fasted—and prayed. Entraining towards midnight, we reached Zeitoun in the small hours of the morning and, scorning sleep, spent the remainder of the night profitably in a steak and eggs canteen.

We sunned ourselves in the soft warmth of the Egyptian winter morning, and ejected from our clothing most of our "companions" in the evacuation, meantime discussing our future movements.

THE LAST NIGHT

"Don't block the way there, file on quickly; this isn't a picture show!"

The snapped-out command came from a Naval officer standing on the end of the little sandbag and planking jetty.   The momentary delay over, the Bushman stepped off the pier into the little row boat, one of a long string with a tug at the seaward end, and sank in a huddled heap in its stern. Almost immediately the tug went ahead and the shore slowly receded.

Was it really over.   All of the Regiment was off, anyway, because he had seen the Colonel step in and *he* had brought up the rear.   And someone had said something about a picture show.   Some parts of the whole show might make good pictures; the essence of a man's brain couldn't be put on to a film though.   They couldn't photograph his thoughts and feelings when the Sergeant told him he would be in the last party of all, the "C3," or those of the fellows who wanted to buy his place in it.   Funny, too, those mates who had gone the previous night never expecting to see him again, and who, all the same, wanted to swap places.   It seemed ages since they went, and yet it was only nine hours or so since "C3" filed along the forward tunnel and took up their listening posts in Wilson's Outlook.

Some cynic must have named that post.   Why, where he had crouched alert, but shivering, for eight out the nine hours, the dirt thrown over on Jacko's side blocked all view, unless you put your head and shoulders over the parapet.   And Jacko's bullets only had eight yards to travel. Eight hours within eight yards of them.   Still, hours had passed without a shot being fired, and cramped and shivering he had crouched alongside of his mate listening for the faintest sound of Turkish activity. The monotony of that had been maddening, and they had blessed the sniper who thought he had found a loophole, and who for a couple of hours put about three shots a minute into some sandbags on the parados. His mate had whispered that the cow fired every time a different louse bit him, and after calculating for a time he came to the conclusion that no cuckoo could spare that Jacko sniper any.

Then the monotony of the shots and the resulting trickle of earth out of the ripped sandbags became worse than the silence. Midnight came. Only 2½ hours to go. A slight humming noise came faintly to his ears. The very trench itself seemed to shudder in sympathy with the tremor of his brain and body as he realized that a Jacko aeroplane was moving directly along and low down over the whole position. Well, if they had spotted anything it would soon have been over, anyway, at the worst a long rest alongside the others, at the best, Constantinople. What would happen to the graves if they did get off? Thank heaven, Bill had been buried at sea.

God! it was cold; his tunic was frosted. They couldn't have their coats; nothing to carry away with them but a couple of Mills bombs in case of accidents before they got off. He must move to take the cramp out of his legs; just a couple of steps and then back alongside his mate. Hours were slowly passing; why, it was just on two o'clock and he could hear the Sergeant creeping along the trench, his muffled feet making a peculiar swishing noise.

"You two go back into Chatham's now," he whispered. "You'll be the only ones there; 'C2' party is just pulling out. One of you take from the tunnel round towards Ryrie's, and the other towards the Beach Line. Watch the saps closely and take a look over now and again. It's pretty quiet."

They had lost no time getting back to Chatham's Post. Thank heaven they could move about there, and an occasional look over was a relief after the unutterable strain of eight hours listening. And only half an hour to go. Minutes passed, and meeting his mate at the tunnel mouth, they had heard the soft footfalls coming along from Wilson's Outlook.

They had fallen in on the rear of the now quickly-moving, yet noiseless, single file, and rapidly and unerringly made their way to "B" Depot. And now they were off, all of them; infantry and all must be off by now.

But all that wouldn't go on pictures. Why, his best mate was buried somewhere about here, the tug might be right over his ocean grave. And some of the best and bravest who lay in shallow graves; all the blood and sweat of the past seven months, and greatest of all, the brotherhood incarnate of mateship, were back there, and no picture show would be game to go there to-morrow.

A mighty explosion woke the Bushman from his fitful sleep. Quinn's Post had gone skyward.

CHAPTER IV

The Days of Romani

THE following day the Regiment marched out for Maadi, and by nightfall its strength of 26 officers and 257 other ranks had been established in the old camp.

A large number of reinforcements, who had arrived too late to take part in the Gallipoli campaign, were stationed there, and during the ensuing few days the re-organization of the Regiment proceeded apace. All hope of a short rest was speedily disposed of. We had arrived at Maadi on the 27th of December; on the last day of the year training re-commenced. The strength of the Regiment had been completed with the pick of a large number of reinforcements, and the body of unabsorbed men, with the squadron of the 12th Regiment, which still remained attached, were formed into a details depot, the total strength of the Regiment amounting to, at one period, over 1,000. Numbers of old hands kept gradually returning from Egyptian hospitals, Malta and England. Certain undesirables were quietly sent to the Detail Camp and we knew them no more. But a large number of first-class men, for whom there was no room in the Regiment, transferred to other units, chiefly the new infantry battalions and artillery brigades then being formed.

"Lloyd Lindsay" Section, Maadi Sports, January 1916.

Maadi Sports, January, 1916. 6th Regiment Team winning Final of Tug-of-War event.

The Regiment had also become considerably over-strength in officers, due to promotions on Gallipoli, vice men who eventually returned, and to a number who had come over in charge of reinforcements. Inevitably some had to drop out, and here the Regiment lost some capable and promising men.

During our seven months' absence the horses had been well cared for. Many reallotments had to be made, and by the opening of the New Year the most profitable period of the Regiment's training was in full swing. Up till now we had had no chance of fulfilling our destiny as mounted soldiers. That was close at hand, and as if realizing it unconsciously, officers and men threw themselves vigorously into the new training. The obvious result was the singular individual and corporate efficiency which characterized those Light Horse Regiments to whom fell the initial pioneering work in the Desert of Sinai.

Competition everywhere was keen, from squadrons to individual sections; and probably the outstanding feature of the general efficiency was the work of sections and their leaders in such tasks of reconnaissance, outpost, flank and screen work. Meantime Maadi became the same home as in former days. January quickly passed away, and early in February rumours of an impending move became rife. These proved correct and during the night of the 24-25th the Regiment rode out, and entraining at Aub-el-Ela station, proceeded to Serapeum, the last party arriving there at 7.45

p.m.   A couple of days were spent in placing the
new camp in order, and training was resumed.   But
training at Maadi and Serapeum proved to be two
different matters.   Speedily the weather became
intensely hot.   Drill had to be done mostly in loose
sand, khamseens made life unbearable, and beyond
the occasional swims in the Suez Canal, relaxa-
tion of any sort was nil.   Even at meal times the
monotony was varied very little. An anathematized
institution—the Regimental cookhouse—was still
in existence, and a few miserable Greek canteens
only supplied inferior goods at extortionate prices.
The Regiment had to learn by years of experience,
the ideal way to feed a body of men.   As may be
imagined, the seven weeks' sojourn at Serapeum
did not carry many pleasant memories when we
rode out for Salhia on the 4th of April.

Passing through Ismailia, we camped the first
night at Moascar.   Leaving early next morning,
we reached Salhia shortly after midday.   Several
days were spent in fixing horse lines and the camp
generally.   Training was continued, but the end
of training days was at hand.   Rumours came
through of the happenings across the Canal, and
at midday on the 23rd of April, 1916, we started
on the long ride, which began at Salhia and ended
two and a half years later, on the Tablelands of
Moab.   Our baptismal day on trek was excessively
hot, and few there were who did not feel like a
good night's rest when Kantara was reached at
sundown.   But nothing like that was in store.
Horses were watered and fed; so were we; and

The Regiment moving from Serapeum to Salhia, April, 1916.

F

Regimental Horse Lines, Salhia, April, 1916.

at 10 o'clock we clanked across the pontoon bridge
and headed for Hill 70.   Arriving there horses
were picketed and men snatched what sleep they
could for a few hours.   Starting again well before
daylight, we left the light metalled road and
entered the trackless desert of Sinai.   A little
after midday we reached the railhead and remained there for the rest of the day and
the succeeding night.   The horses had not
had water since the previous evening at Kantara,
and the water-bottles were getting very low.   A
scanty supply of precious liquid was obtained from
the railhead, but the horses mostly had to spend
their first day in Sinai unwatered.   Strong outposts
were placed round the bivouac area during the
night, and shortly after daylight the Regiment
moved out for Romani.   We knew that some mis-
fortune had befallen a Yeomanry Brigade somewhere in the locality.   Before long we passed a
column coming in.   They wore a dejected air, the
reason of which we were not long finding out.
Two hours later we rode into a deserted camp at
Romani, where everything stood just as it had
been left.   From a couple of shallow brackish
wells we watered our thirsty horses, and during
the remainder of that day we established our camp
on the eastern slope of the Hod.   We had come to
a war once more.

The Hod at Romani lay in a depression at the
south-eastern corner, and inside a chain of giant
sand hills.   By the time the outposts had dragged
themselves and their gear through the heavy sand

to positions commanding the approaches to the
camp, and everyone had done the usual "stand to"
the following morning, there seemed to be no
doubt that the war was still on, and the dead
bodies of a Yeomanry trooper and his horse, just
outside the semicircle of hills, grimly emphasized
the fact.

On the morning of the 27th the Regiment moved
out for Katia and Oghritina. The 7th Regiment
had, on the previous day, patrolled to Katia and
recovered several wounded Yeomen. With screen
and flank guards in position, C Squadron of the
Regiment passed to the north of Katia and made
straight for Oghritina. For the first time we had
a job for which we had trained; the carrying out
of an armed reconnaissance into enemy territory.
Few realized the awful spectacle waiting on the
sandhills between the Hods of Oghritina. Several
dead Turks lay in the path of the screen as it
floundered up the loose sand dune. But dotted at
intervals among the wild confusion of the rifled
camp, lay the remains of numbers of the
Yeomanry who had fallen in the action four
days previously. Some had been partially
buried. In a little shallow redoubt close to the
camp lay at least a dozen bodies. Fully fifty
lay around the top of the hill, and numerous
dead Turks showed that the little Yeomanry garrison had put up a good show till overwhelmed by
heavy odds. Someone had obviously blundered.
The topography of the ridge between the two hods
was such, that a well-entrenched battalion would

Romani

El Male

have had no light task in holding the position against the body of Turks, estimated at 4,000, which had attacked it on the 23rd. To the north and south-east the steepness of the sand dunes formed a slight barrier, but to hold these points and also gently sloping ground to the west and south meant spreading the little Yeomanry force —a squadron and a half—along a defence line of at least a mile. On the other hand, to concentrate as they had, and they could do little else, in a small cup-like hollow on the hill top, made their annihilation a certainty, and the Turkish attack coming from all quarters, and finally, judging from the bodies, up the gentle rise to the south could hardly fail.

Such was the picture of death and desolation that greeted the eyes of C Squadron's screen. Search was immediately made in neighbouring hods and it resulted in the discovery of three wounded men—two Yeomanry and one Turk. Two were able to ride back to Romani, but one of the Yeomen had a badly fractured leg. Sufficient material was obtained from the remains of the camp to improvise a stretcher, and working in reliefs, A and C Squadrons carried him the whole way back to Romani.

The Regiment now settled down to one of the hardest phases of its career. Both horses and men were more or less soft. No training includes learning to quench a raging thirst with brackish water. A series of wells were sunk in the locality, but with few exceptions, they were brackish to a nauseating degree. Gradually the camel transport system became organized and fantasse water was supplied in small quantities. The Regiment found outposts with at least half its strength every other night; early reconnoitring patrols and day observation posts, and the monotonous regularity of the early morning "stand to" became painful.

The 5th Regiment had been stationed at Dueidar since the crossing of the Canal, so the whole of the pioneering work of the first month in Sinai —the exploration, well sinking, reconnoitring dashes—devolved upon the 6th and 7th. On the 7th of May the Regiment moved out to reconnoitre Bir-el-Abd, which was supposed to be a camping place of forward Turkish patrols. Leaving Romani in the afternoon we reached Katia early, fed up and watered there. Moving on again shortly after dark we arrived at Oghritina and stood by our horses there till daybreak, then moving on again towards Bir el Abd. Signs of a recent camp were visible there, but what was much more welcome was the old stone well with its plentiful supply of soft water. We "boiled up" and shortly afterwards moved back by Oghritina and Katia to Romani, reaching camp at 7 p.m. Outposts as usual.

Life speedily became one stunt after another. The small daily patrols kept us from forgetting the bigger weekly ones, and the next big one never needed any effort of memory to remember it. A

Watering Horses at Bir-el-Abd.

draft of 29 other ranks, under Lieut. O. W.
Tooth, marched in on the 13th inst, and on the
afternoon of the 15th the Regiment moved out on
the famous Bayoud stunt. The day had been intensely hot. By 9 p.m. we had reached Sagia, halt-
ing and feeding up at Katia on the way. But the
desert night, instead of cooling down considerably,
remained at furnace heat. Outposting around
Sagia that night we sat coatless and hatless and
few there were who did not begin the following
day with an already parched throat, for we knew
that until we reached Katia on the return journey
there was no certainty of any water being obtained,
and one bottle a man only was carried.

Daylight found us well on the way to Bayoud.
From sunrise the heat was intense and the air stagnant. The sand dunes became almost impassable
mountains; we climbed up on foot and slid down
the other side. A tantalizing glimpse of a Turkish camel patrol disappearing over a distant skyline was the only sign of the enemy. By nine
o'clock the advance guard reached the Hod-el-
Bayoud, finding, besides a number of wells and
some troughing, sufficient indication that the camp
had been hurriedly abandoned. But only the advance squadron reached Bayoud and luxuriated
momentarily in its sweet-well water. The remainder halted a mile or so from the Hod, and
about ten o'clock the return journey was begun.
The heat was now frightful. The morning stillness had gone. A stiff breeze like a blast from the
fiery furnace broke the sand peaks into quasi-

volcanic action. It blasted the already desperately
thirsty men and horses and rendered the few
drops of bottle water that remained undrinkable.
Steadily we moved back towards Sagia, the screen
and flank guards exploring every handy hod in the
vain hope of finding water.   The sand dunes
seemed to become more and more mountain like,
the miles seemed to become leagues.   We rested
a few minutes in a hod half way and then pushed
on to Sagia where we knew there was a small well.
At last we rode in to Sagia.   Alas! the supply was
a mere trickle, which meant hours to water men
alone, besides the already frantic horses. Colonel
Fuller took charge of the well and speedily reduced what was fast becoming a rabble to an
orderly parade, but it was a case of *sauve qui
peut.*

Seeing the length of time it would take to water
the entire Regiment, numbers of men obtained
permission to ride on to Katia, about four miles
distant, where the supply was unlimited.   In
parties of two or more they rode doggedly along
towards the distant patch of grey-green that
marked the Katia Oasis.   The horses, realizing
equally with their riders that a last effort was
necessary, plugged along gamely, and after two
hours agony were rewarded.   Bucket after bucket
was drawn up from the old stone well, horses and
men drank side by side, and when at last the
raging demon had been quenched the horses were
unsaddled, washed, and led into the shade of the
Hod and tempted with their nosebags.   But the

Burning Captured Enemy Material at Hod-el-Bayoud, May 16, 1916.

effort for many had been too great. Lying down they rested with closed eyes as if trying to forget the nightmare of the previous 24 hours. The Regiment gradually strung back towards sundown into Katia, and reached camp at Romani by degrees during the evening. The reaction at Sagia proved too much for numbers. On the following day four officers, Major O'Brien, Capt. Ryrie, Lieuts. Pearce and Hedley, and eleven other ranks were admitted to hospital suffering from sunstroke or heat exhaustion. The Field Ambulance had been stationed at Katia during the day. Its thermometer, placed at midday under a palm thatch, registered 122 degrees!

BAYOUD

The sands of the desert seemed to be continually getting hotter, to say nothing of the winds. The water was more brackish, and stunts longer, and the palm hods scarcer and scantier; or, so it seemed to the Bushman as he saddled up on the afternoon of that 15th of May. Just what this stunt was no one was exactly certain, possibly the usual all-night ride, and a dash at daybreak on a Turkish outpost, then a burning and exhausting ride back to Romani with a night cossack post to follow. But the heat promised to be a record, and ominous warnings about looking after the contents of water-bottles pointed to an extra dry stunt.

*　　*　　*　　*　　*　　*

By nine o'clock the following morning "halt"
and "dismount" had been given and the squadrons
in support sat in their horses' shade and vainly
tried to keep the weary and thirsty beasts from
moving. The advance squadron was all right, it
had gone on to Bayoud and filled itself with a
water supply like a camel. The march from Sagia,
the overnight outpost camp, had begun at daylight, and the atmosphere of the early morning
hours had hung fetid and stagnant, like a pall
over the giant sand dunes.

The Bushman's horse moved. Cursing, silently,
he shifted into the new patch of shade and took
the cork out of his water-bottle. On reflection he
put it back again. There was less than half a
bottle and they would certainly never get back to
Katia before well into the afternoon. There
might be the chance of a "boil up," he had tea;
not that it would take much boiling, but a mouthful of tea would be worth the lot as it was now.

He noticed a tiny whisp of sand rising on the
sand peak against which they had halted, and
mechanically he reflected that the wind was rising.
Anything seemed better than the awful stillness
of the burning air, yet if the wind rose much the
blast off a bush fire would be nothing to it. Ah,
the officers were mounting. The Bushman swung
into the saddle and followed his wheeling troop
round in the direction of home. He looked at his
watch. A quarter past ten; perhaps they would
halt at Sagia. There was a well there, but a very
poor one; if he only got a chance to make his drop

of tea, he didn't care much if he didn't get a drink till Katia. But the poor old horse floundering up the loose sand of the hillsides, he would have to suffer.

The wind was rising fast. At intervals in the sea of burning sand the precipitous sides of the dunes were veiled by a creeping, shimmering film moving gently upwards and rising in little spiral wreaths several feet high from the pointed peaks. And, occasionally, as the blast grew fiercer, the whole razor-backs broke into sweeping crests of sand which fell into drifts of molten powder on their leeward sides.

The Bushman, riding on the right flank guard, caught a glimpse of a distant hod through the burning shimmering haze of sand. It couldn't be Sagia, he knew. Ah, the directing troop was turning towards it; there *might* be a well there. A quarter of an hour later the flank guard was signalled to close in to the main body, and the Bushman rode into the hod. Men and horses were scattered about getting what scanty shade they could from the lofty palm trees, and the few who had water left in their bottles were busily "boiling up." A small well there certainly was, but the water stank. He saw one or two thirst-mad men take a few mouthfuls only to pay the penalty with a violent attack of nausea. His last drop of bottle-water quickly became strong tea; but, shared with his mates, it meant little more than a few gulps each. He saw men go out to it with sunstroke

G

and exhaustion and others carrying them to shade to await an ambulance cart.

A very brief rest soon ended.   Mounted once more he pushed his horse out on to the flank again. Sagia could not be very far off now, and doggedly horse and man steeled themselves to endure the next few hours.

Sagia at last.   Everyone was struggling towards the well, and many a heart sank as men realized that it would take hours to water both men and horses.   The order was passed round the Bushman's troop for fit men and horses to make to Katia.   Could he do it; two hours more.   But there was plenty there for man and beast, and urging his horse made nearly desperate by the smell of water, he rode out of the hod and headed for Katia.   Others were going too.   Nerved by the companionship, he moved slowly onwards. Hill after hill he crossed, an hour passed and he could see the dark blotch of the palm trees at Katia; or he thought he could.   Might it be a mirage and the well be miles further on.   But the old horse was stepping out gamely; he knew, at any rate, that water was close.   Why now it was quite close.   He could see the old stone well and one or two of the fellows there already drawing up bucket after bucket.   Only a few hundred yards to go.   "Come on, old man, the bucket and the rope is all we want now."   And, side by side at the old stone well, they drank till they could drink no more.

*   *   *   *   *   *

Watering Area, Et Maler.

Truly we were experiencing the limit of climatic conditions. Six months previously we had nearly perished in 26 degrees of frost, now we were enduring the extremities of heat and thirst. But a welcome relief was at hand. On the 22nd, having been relieved by the 1st Brigade, we moved back to Hill 70 and went into reserve. Although by no means a physical or mental paradise, a month in reserve at Hill 70 was very acceptable. Short leave was granted to Port Said and, beyond the usual stables, regimental fatigues and occasional patrols, duties were not excessive.

On the 24th of June we marched out again in the small hours of the morning and proceeding to Bir et Maler, a series of hods close to Romani, relieved a regiment of New Zealand Mounted Rifles camped there. Once more we settled down to the unattractive desert existence of patrols, long and short, night and day, outposts, and well sinking, together with the hundred and one minor duties which fall to the "askari." Twice we made night dashes for Bir el Abd and Bir Salmana. At the latter place we were rewarded with a skirmish with an enemy outpost, but as a general thing he was too wily to be caught, and had only to fall back a few miles to get safely out of reach. The night march over heavy sand always placed the advantage with the enemy's camels when it came to a test of speed. We had practically despaired of ever doing anything more than resultless patrolling and rounding up Bedouins, when the unexpected happened and the enemy came to us on, perhaps, the only occasion save the general attack on Gallipoli on the 19th of May, 1915.

On the 19th of July the Regiment, in conjunction with the rest of the Brigade, which now included the Wellington Mounted Rifles in place of the 5th, moved out for a further reconnaissance of Bir el Abd. A strong Turkish force had put up a remarkable feat in reaching Oghritina unobserved. Our column had passed Katia on its outward march when an aeroplane dropped a message to the effect that the enemy were in strong force at Oghritina. But for this timely information it is certain that the screen at least would have met with casualties, if not disaster. Falling back to Katia the Regiment bivouacked and outposted there for the night. A determined reconnaissance next day showed that the enemy's forward positions covering Oghritina were well advanced, and reached a strong natural position on a ridge behind Hod um Ugba. We withdrew at sundown and arrived back at Romani well towards midnight. It seemed obvious that the enemy was preparing for another desperate attempt to reach the Suez Canal. Also we soon saw that our tactics were calculated to gradually draw him on to Romani, while delaying the final battle as long as possible.

We now began what was probably one of the most strenuous periods in our existence. Working on alternate days with the 1st Brigade our programme was as follows:—Moving out just after

midnight we halted in the big gap known as the
Booby Hatch, the main gateway to the Romani
and Et Maler positions, till dawn.   Thence we
moved on till the screen was pulled up by the
enemy outposts.   Watching and worrying these
outposts, driving them in where possible, flanking demonstrations and occasional attacks on any
positions that appeared to offer any chance of
success.   This was the daily programme until darkness covered our weary withdrawal back to Et
Maler.   And daily we endured the pitiless heat
of midsummer, the eye-racking glare of the never-
ending sand, and an unquenchable thirst.   Yet the
spirits and energy of the Regiment remained un-
checked.   As soon as the returning column passed
a point beyond the earshot of the furthest enemy
outpost, troop after troop broke into a chorus of
song, and the remaining miles back to Et Maler
reminded one of the end of a day's picnic, rather
than the grimness of its actual reality.   On the
28th of June we reached our usual positions beyond Katia, and shortly after midday D Troop of
C Squadron, commanded by Lieut. R. Black,
being then posted on a ridge towards Um Ugba,
received orders to attack the hod in conjunction
with a squadron of the Wellington Mounted
Rifles working on the northern flank.   A well-
timed gallop enabled us to make at least half a
mile of ground.   The enemy fire from the ridges
behind Um Ugba was nullified by the speed with
which we moved, and finally we dismounted for
action behind a rise overlooking the hod, and here

we were joined by a section of our Machine Gun Squadron, under Lieut. Cunningham.

The hod now lay only a few hundred yards below us. It appeared to be occupied by a handful of snipers only, but from the ridges to the east and south, machine gun and rifle fire played on us from a convenient range of about 800 yards. At a concerted signal from the Wellingtons, D Troop advanced in extended order on the hod; Lieut. Cunningham at the same time removing his machine gun to a small eminence which enabled him to reply to the fire opened on to us directly the advance began. Lieut. Cunningham's superb handling of a particularly efficient crew, and his characteristic disregard of personal danger, exposing himself repeatedly to locate targets, was probably our salvation.

Walking quietly along we must have presented a splendid target to the enemy guns on the ridge behind the hod, but repeated bursts from the gun in our rear kept them moderately quiet until when, about a hundred yards from the hod, we doubled for the shelter of the palm trees in the cup-like hollow. Immediately heavy cross fire was directed at us, but we reached the hod with the loss of one man (Trooper R. B. Smith) slightly wounded. The Wellingtons had meantime advanced to the north and were coming through the main hod. About a dozen snipers who had sheltered there retreated as we made the first palm trees. One attempted to make the hill top behind, and was brought down running. The remainder, retreating northwards, were captured by the Wellingtons, and during a double across an open space between the palm groves, our second casualty occurred, Trooper F. J. Collins receiving a bullet in the back. Our machine gun, in spite of two casualties, still gave us splendid covering fire, and the horses had meantime been brought to the western end of the hod. Mounting here, we retired at the gallop, enemy fire again proving ineffectual as we crossed the open ground to our original starting point. The machine gun crew got out with the same careless dash that had characterized them throughout the afternoon. Their horse-holders galloped right to the forward position they occupied, and in a few seconds both gun and crew, followed by a futile stream of fire, had made a safe position further towards Katia.

Upon the withdrawal of the Regiment that evening, a listening post of Corporal R. Thorne and 2 men under Lieut. Pearce, remained behind on a ridge overlooking Hamisah to ascertain any enemy movements during the night. Lieut. Pearce was shot dead at close range by a sniper. Corporal Thorne, discovering his officer to be dead, decided to withdraw. Finding almost immediately that all retreat through Katia was cut off, he plunged into the enemy country to the south of Hamisah. But whenever he attempted to strike a direct course to Romani, strong Turkish patrols blocked the way. By dint of riding all night, and by superb bushmanship, he succeeded, in spite of several hairbreadth escapes, in bringing his party right round the flank towards Dueidar, eventually making to Hill 70 by 9 a.m. Lieut. Pearce's body was recovered next day and brought to Et Maler for interment.

The same tactics continued—24 hours in and 24 hours out of camp—and each day the enemy advance came gradually closer. By the 3rd of August they had taken possession of Katia and Hamisah and the ridges on either flank, and a general battle seemed inevitable. We reached our camp that evening at nine o'clock, praying alternately for a good night's sleep and for the speedy culmination of the fortnight's constant strain. The latter came a few hours later. Awakened partially by the sound of distant rifle fire, and thoroughly a few moments later by the order to "stand to," we turned out at 12.30 a.m., and made ready for the events of the day. Holding our horses and formed up ready to move out, we dozed till 4 a.m., while the gradual approach of intermittent rifle fire to the south warned us that the day had arrived.

At 4 a.m. the whole Regiment mounted, and moving out at the gallop went to the support of the 1st Brigade, which had been bearing the brunt of the attack since midnight. In less than a mile S.E. of Et Maler we dismounted for action, and advancing several hundred yards on foot under heavy fire, rifle, machine gun and shrapnel, took up a line which we held against repeated attacks till 7 a.m. The enemy appeared to be having things much his own way. All around Romani and Et Maler positions his artillery roared, aeroplanes, unopposed, bombed our camps, led-horses and railhead depots, to their own sweet will; ineffectively, nevertheless, thanks mainly to the heavy sand. The 1st Brigade withdrew at the gallop shortly after 7 o'clock, and when soon afterwards our firing-line dropped back to the led horses and we also mounted, and pursued by heavy shelling galloped out and away towards the railway line, the ordinary man in the ranks might have been pardoned for imagining that Jacko had scored a bit of a win.

But an inspiring figure had been amongst us all the morning, and with such a leader how *could* we lose. Brig.-Gen. Royston had taken command of our Brigade on the departure of General Ryrie for England in June. "Galloping Jack," as he was popularly called, came to us with a reputation, and never did leader make good or enhance a reputation like he on that 4th day of August. Wherever the fire was hottest, wherever a word of command, or the sight of his heroic figure, a cheery word of encouragement, or the example of his extraordinary dash and courage were required, General Royston appeared at the opportune moment. None of those whom he led that day can ever remember him without that thrill which makes every good soldier know that it was worth while.

By nine o'clock we had occupied a new position to the right of Wellington Ridge and gradually the tactics of our retirement became apparent.

Drawn on by our withdrawal the attacking force
had attempted to cross the precipitous sand
mountains towards the railway line, while their
efforts to reach our camp at Romani and Et Maler
had been completely held up. A large force was
quietly allowed to occupy a hod almost surrounded
by steep sand hills where they were compelled to
remain by our frontal fire and a barrage of shrapnel in their rear. Heat, thirst and exhaustion now
had their effect. Threatened on their western
flank by a regiment of New Zealanders and a body
of Scottish Infantry coming up from Kantara,
they gave up the unequal struggle and hoisted the
white flag. Even at this dramatic moment General
Royston appeared then, as always, at the gallop,
and never a throat among us that was too
cracked to cheer as he disappeared in a cloud of
sand. At sundown we advanced a short distance
on foot finally taking up a position where we outposted for the night, the led horses being brought
up close under cover of darkness.

Daylight found us again in the saddle, and advancing towards Katia by a route which circled to
the south. The enemy had, during the night,
decided on a general retirement. We soon came
into touch with his rear guard, which made a very
half-hearted attempt to stay our progress. Each
hod yielded up its complement of prisoners;
abandoned wounded freely marked the line of retreat, and the dead on Wellington Ridge testified
to the effectiveness of the delaying action of the
previous day. At Hod el Ene our largest capture

took place, three hundred of the exhausted and demoralized enemy surrendering without firing a shot. Our advance towards Katia continued till midday. The sweltering heat was merciless; what wonder, after the happenings of the previous fortnight, capped by the just-gone twenty-four hours, that physically, the Regiment, both horses and men, was near breaking point. The horses suffered worst. They had had nothing to drink since the evening of the 3rd inst; we at least had started the battle of Romani with one full waterbottle. Few felt inclined for such food as remained in the haversacks. And the most trying time of the whole strenuous fortnight was yet to come. We had to wait. It mattered not why, but for several hours we crouched under our horses, taking, when possible, advantage of their shadows, the only shade available in a wilderness of burning sand.

At two o'clock the welcome order to mount was passed along, and we moved off to take part in a general attack upon Katia. The long straggling hod was evidently strongly held by the Turkish rear guard, and the flanks from Hamisah to Hill 245 were almost impregnable owing to the numerous sandbag redoubts built by the Turkish army during its occupation of Katia. Five mounted Brigades took part in the general assault: the 1st, 2nd and 3rd L.H. Brigades, the New Zealand Mounted Rifle Brigade and the 5th Brigade of Mounted Yeomanry. Dismounting two miles from Katia and directly opposite the main hod, the Regiment advanced, at first steadily, and finally in short rushes. The enemy guns sought vainly for our led horses, but the machine guns and rifles concealed on the edge of the hod played effectively on our ranks as we doubled across the dry swampy ground fronting the oasis. We reached a small line of sand eminences several hundred yards from our objective and waited there preparatory to making the final assault. But it all depended on the success of the flanking attack towards Hamisah, and this failed. All credit to the tactics of the Turks and their determination at all costs not to be outflanked. For in the now pitiable condition of semi-exhaustion our men found themselves in, it was impossible to carry Katia by a direct frontal attack. For several hours we lay behind the sparsest of cover and returned when possible the resolute fire of the Turkish machine guns. Towards sundown, the inevitable happened, a withdrawal was ordered, and just prior to retiring Colonel Fuller was wounded. It seemed as if the withdrawal must be attended with heavy loss. Many men were too exhausted to do anything but walk slowly away from Katia, and parties carrying wounded men moved under fire for upwards of half a mile. But the sun was now setting behind us, and made a blur of the weary and dispirited figures making their way slowly to where the led horses had been left. More than anything though, our safety was made possible by the heroic work of Lieut. Cunningham and his machine guns. With his usual disregard

of personal safety, he posted his guns in commanding positions, and during the hottest fire coolly
superintended their effective use.

Shortly after dark the Regiment had re-
assembled and started back for Et Maler. Both
horse and men seemed to make a final call on their
waning resources of endurance. But the horses,
first at the water troughs and later with their nosebags, found life worth living again, and the men
soon briefly forgot in the oblivion of sleep the
agonies of the last two days. The total casualties
for the 4th and 5th of August amounted to 7
killed and 45 wounded, of which several died
later, including Sgt. M. Johnston, of Molong,
N.S.W., who in death, as in life, set an everlasting
example to his Regiment.

KATIA

It was midday.

The column halted in a cup-like depression a
couple of miles from the long straggling hod. The
order passed to dismount, and, lying on the burning sand on the shady side of his horse, the Bushman shook his empty water-bottle and wondered
what the afternoon would bring. Since daybreak
they had advanced from behind Et Maler on the
heels of the beaten Turkish Army, exploring hods,
collecting prisoners, and praying for water. The
last fortnight had been severe enough, but yesterday was the limit, and to-day—well, whatever
happened he hoped it wouldn't be delayed.

They were winning, anyway. Jacko was going

for his life and how must the poor devils have
suffered.   Every possy they passed was littered
with green date peelings, and the prisoners they
took looked like hunted devils.   What on earth
was the waiting for?   They had been there an
hour now, literally frying on the sand.   He knew
they were going to attack Katia.   Plenty of water
there, and probably a strong Turkish rear guard.
But this infernal waiting was taking the last remnants of vitality out of everyone.   He thought of
something long, drawn through ice, if he ever
went on leave again.   He could hear a couple of
chaps rowing over their horses disturbing each
others' shade.   They were agreeing to settle the
argument after they had settled the Jackos.   They
were mates, too.   Well, it was enough to make
any man quarrel with his best friend, this infernal
waiting on top of everything else.   But no sign of
a move.   Some Jacko guns were thundering from
behind Katia, and he could see shrapnel bursting
away towards the left flank.   There seemed to be
no one over towards Hamisah.   Perhaps they were
waiting for another Brigade to come up.

Thank God the front of the column was mounting.   Swinging out into artillery formation they
moved quietly towards Katia.   Crossing the first
skyline was enough to draw shrapnel, but a steady
gallop, screened by the hollows between dunes and
a scanty hod or two, brought them safely to the
series of little sandhills fronting the dry swamp
behind which lay Katia.

A few minutes later the Bushman found himself

part of an extended line doubling from one sand-hill to another and wondering why more men didn't go down. Jacko had evidently plenty of machine guns planted in Katia, and from the burst of his shrapnel away to the rear it looked as though he had located the horses. They were now on the edge of the dry swamp. It was a good half-mile to the first palm trees and the only cover worth talking about was a small outcrop of sand running parallel to the hod. Two or three hundred yards away it was. The men who got there would be lucky. Ah, they were off again. The ground was hard; better to run on. They were going down now; the man on his right pitched forward on to his face; and, glancing along the extended line as he ran, he could see figures lying still and others trying to crawl or limp back to the shelter of the sandhills they had just left.

That was close. Flecks of dirt spattered up all round him. Another minute and he lay panting behind the friendly shelter of the last cover they would get before the final assault. He turned his head to watch the second line coming up. Continuous bursts of machine gun fire were following them all the way. They had got the range properly now. A sergeant was making towards him; another twenty yards and he would be safe. Ah, they had got him, and it looked like for keeps. The Bushman joined in the rush of several others and dragged the sergeant in behind the nearest sandhill.

* * * * * *

H

"How in hell are we going to carry him out?"

"On our rifles and crossed arms. Two on each side, one take his head and the other his legs. Now, lift him steadily and keep in step as much as possible. Make straight for the sandhill."

They had padded the rifles as best they could. But no matter how carefully they stepped they knew that every movement cost the silent figure untold agony. Yet not quite silent. The wounded man spoke as they started: "You fellows are Britons to stick to a man like this."

Walking almost on each other's spurs and cramped by their necessarily crouching attitude, the huddled group of men moved at a snail's pace for the nearest shelter. They crossed the dry swamp almost unmolested. The sun was setting and its flickering rays dancing on the background of red sandhills blurred them as a target. But as they struggled up the first ridge the sand spat about their feet and the quiet figure spoke again.

"Put me down behind the hill and send a sand-cart after dark. Six of you make a big target, you know," and in a whisper as they struggled on, "It's good to have mates like you chaps."

*   *   *   *   *   *

In the British Military Cemetery of Old Cairo stands a monument erected by his comrades to one of the bravest of the brave—Sergeant Major Johnston.

*   *   *   *   *   *

For two days we rested, buried our dead and
collected from the battlefield any gear abandoned
by the enemy.   On the afternoon of the 8th we
moved out once more in pursuit of the enemy, now
retreating everywhere, but concentrated in force
at Bir el Abd.

Leaving Katia at 10 p.m. we moved forward to
take part in a strong reconnaissance of Bir el Abd.
An attempt was made to encircle the position.
The 3rd L.H. Brigade operated from the south,
the New Zealand Brigade from the west, the 2nd
Brigade from the north, and the 1st Brigade, it
possible, was to menace the position from the east.
Less than an hour after sunrise the following
morning the action started.   Accompanied by the
Ayrshire Battery, the 2nd Brigade approached its
position by daylight and was warmly welcomed by
a series of 4.7 H.E.'s bursting in close proximity
to the column.   As reserve to the Brigade, the
Regiment,   now   under   Major   Bruxner,   was
stationed several hundred yards south of the Ayrshire Battery's position.   All day long the
Battery waged a vigorous duel with the enemy's
4.7 and shrapnel, and one unlucky direct hit put
several teams of horses, a gun, and its crew out of
action.   Vainly the enemy tried to locate our led
horses, but although several high explosives came
very close, we suffered no material damage.   A
general attack took place at 11 a.m. and the New
Zealand Brigade was drawn into an awkward
position during a heavy encounter.   To assist in
their withdrawal during the afternoon, the Regi-

ment went into action, and finally covered the withdrawal of the badly knocked about Ayrshire
Battery.   We withdrew to Oghritina where we
drew rations and forage and bivouacked for the
night.

Returning to Khirba next day we found the
deserted Turkish camp to contain some very
acceptable articles of loot.   Barley for the horses
was plentiful, and besides tea, dates, meal and
olives, there were several hundredweights of
dried apricots pressed into rolls like brown paper.
Under the comprehensive name of "mungaree"
we learnt during the next few days to envy the
Turks its possession as a ration issue.   For two
days we remained at Khirba, and here we said
farewell to "Galloping Jack."   In a brief address
he bade us good-bye from the saddle, and his exit
in a cloud of dust over a sandhill and followed by
deafening cheers, was truly characteristic of our
brief but unforgettable experience of his leadership.

From Bir el Abd to Katia we saw evidence of
the great difficulty the enemy had had in trans-
porting his heavy artillery through the heavy sand.
Besides temporary roads of brambles, they had
used some thousands of feet of 9 by 2 inch planking, placing it in front of the guns and moving
them along with what must have been snail-like,
if sure, progress.   But what can be said of the
great feat of the Turkish Infantry.   We, on horse-
back, knew what it was to campaign during the
desert midsummer.   Their secret march to Oghri-

tina unobserved by aerial patrols was in itself remarkable enough, but their sufferings during the
weeks culminating in the battles of Romani and
Katia must have been intense. On foot, carrying
full infantry gear, living partly on green dates,
and during the last two days waterless, their effort
to drive us from Romani was, in spite of failure,
such as to rouse the utmost admiration amongst
their conquerors.

The enemy were now in full retreat eastwards
of Salmana, and for the time being our acquaint-
ance with him was ended. Withdrawing via Katia
we returned to Et Maler on the 13th of August,
and for the rest of the month, both horses and
men enjoyed a badly-needed rest. The casualty
list of sickness and death made a number of vacan-
cies amongst the officers, and the following were
promoted to commissioned rank:—Sig. Sgt. J.
Back, Sgts. Allman, Ronald, Lomax and Corp. H.
Dickson.   Popular also were the captaincys of
Lieuts. Thompson, Tooth S., and Close.   The
worst of the summer heat had now passed, and
horses were beginning to be inured to the hardships of desert life. But a number had succumbed
to the strain; sand colic and sore backs were the
predominant ailments, and many had to be evacuated to Veterinary Hospitals and replaced by re-
mounts. We left Et Maler on the 11th of September and, moving by Katia, reached our new
camping area, Hod el Hasaniya, the same afternoon.   Lieut.-Col. Fuller returned three days
later having recovered from his wound, and again

took charge of the Regiment. Preparations
were soon on foot for an attack on the Turkish
position at El Mazar.

Moving out at 2.30 a.m. on the morning of the
16th we marched to Hod el Ge'eila, where we
camped for the day. Sundown found us on the
move again and joined up with the 3rd Brigade
and the Inverness and Ayrshire Batteries on the
Mazar Road, four miles east of Salmana. A
tedious all-night ride was followed by an equally
wearisome day. A Squadron of the Regiment
remained posted six miles from Mazar, in event of
a covering force being required during a possible
retirement. C Squadron had a wildly exciting
time as artillery escort, and the remainder of the·
Regiment was in reserve. After a half-hearted
and ineffectual attempt on the Turkish positions,
the column withdrew, and a heart-breaking journey back to Salmana commenced. For no very
apparent reason, the Mazar stunt is usually admitted to have been one of the most wearisome
desert rides we ever experienced. Perhaps the
knowledge of the utter futility of the whole ex-
pedition permeated the parched throats and
weighted the aching bodies with the last straw.
It was a still weary Regiment that withdrew the
following morning to Hasaniya and settled down
to holding part of the front line. Alternately
squadrons camped at Homossia, linking up with
the Camel Corps and the 3rd Brigade on the right
and left respectively. But we were not long to
sweeten our outpost and front line work with ripe

dates moist with the desert fog of early morning. On the 29th we marched out again, proceeding by Romani, where we stayed a day, moved back to Hill 70, which we reached by the 2nd of October. Here we settled down in reserve. Training, sport, an occasional patrol or detached duty, and leave to Alexandria and Port Said; such was the programme for the following six weeks.

Football came very much into favour during our spell at Hill 70. Contests between troops and squadrons finally culminated into inter-regimental matches. The standard in the Regiment soon reached that. excellence which hardly ever deteriorated during its front line career. Most of the players came from C Squadron, which, throughout, supplied the bulk of the Regiment's athletes. Prominent among the footballers at this period were Holt Hardy, Billy Weir, Clive Capel, Steve Brown, Neil Ross, "Snow" Lester, Bruce Webb, the brothers Lowe, Rock, Fred Walker, Sedgwick, Artie Reynolds, Joe Nevitt, Noel Dowling, the brothers Fenner and Lester Meares. We beat the 5th Regiment at Duiedar and lost to the 7th, but the game had taken a firm hold and during the ensuing winter months did much to liven the monotony of desert life and keep men in a fit condition.

CHAPTER V

The Promised Land

TOWARDS the end of November the Regiment left Hill 70, and travelling by Romani and Khirba, reached Bayoud on the 25th inst. C Squadron, under Major Ferguson, took over a detached post at Mageibra, and the remainder of the Regiment established itself at Bayoud. Settling down to the same old desert life we passed the midwinter months at these two posts. Stationed as we were on the extreme flank of the line, a great deal of patrolling to outlying points, day observation posts and night outposts, formed the main points of our programme.

From Bayoud, A and B Squadrons despatched patrols daily to Geisi, Wilegha, Bir Jameil and Rueishe, and from Mageibra C Squadron supplied them to Aweyda, Hill 484 and Bada. Reconnaissances in force were also carried out to El Barga and El Rakwa, Hamaiyir, and in conjunction with three sections of the I.C.C., through Zagadan.

The weather towards the New Year, and early in January, became very inclement. Rain fell on Christmas Day, and while its quantity was not great it was sufficient to make the hessian bivvies of the men inhabitable only with great difficulty. The nights became intensely cold, and sand storms blew with hurricane force, often partially covering

New Year Sports, Bayoud, 1917.

Signal Station, Zagadan.

an outpost during its hours of attempted sleep. But notwithstanding, both health and spirits rose with the cold weather. Canteen supplies became available, and together with parcels from home, and issues from the Comforts' Fund, combined to make the Christmas of 1916 compare very favourably with any other. Football was vigorously revived, particularly in C Squadron. It almost became compulsory for everyone to play, as many as six squadron teams taking part in a local Mageibra competition. And the squadron reached the height of its success by first drawing with, and then beating, the 7th Regiment, by 3 to nil on their ground at Hassaniya, Noel Dowling scoring after a magnificent run from behind half way.

As the month of January wore on, news of Magdabah, El Arish and Rafa began to make the Regiment restless, and it was with delight that, after a short stay at Hasaniya, we marched out on the 2nd of February for the gradually extending front line which by now had crept well beyond El Arish. We moved via Moseifig to Mazar, where we camped for five days. Thence we trekked to Masaid, and camped near the beach close to several other Brigades, who were spelling after their successful dashes on Rafa and Magdabah. For eleven days we remained at Masaid. A good deal of time was devoted to mounted training in tactics calculated to repel cavalry attacks and safely negotiate shrapnel barrages. A few minor patrols had to be found but most ranks found time to enjoy the surf and a series of football matches.

Towards the end of our stay at Masaid, Major H. D. White returned from leave to Australia and was posted to the Regiment as 2nd in command. Lieut. R. Black was admitted to hospital, Lieut. Hardy reported to the School of Instruction, Zeitoun, and Lieut. Britten returned from detached duty with Brigade Headquarters.

On the 22nd of February we moved out for our final trek in Sinai. Practically from the time of leaving Bir Salmana the country had very gradually improved. The bare sand mountains of Romani and Bayoud, the sparsely scrubbed hills of Oghritina and Bir el Abd, had changed. The scrub had grown denser, the occasional long, rough desert grass became more frequent, new herbages appeared, and even clusters of spring flowers waved alongside the old road, that eloquent epic of the history of the world. Older by far than the world's most ancient landmarks, the old caravan route had throughout countless ages marked the march of conquering armies and the fleeing of defeated hosts. The most ancient legions had followed its path, Assyrian, Persian, Roman and Saracen, in turn, had camped in its wayside hods. Napoleon had led his victorious hosts along it from Egypt to Syria, and now the latest born of the world's armies had signalized its crossing of the dividing line between "desert and strown," by the victory of Rafa.

We reached Sheikh Zowaid early in the afternoon. The sand had become firmer and occasional wheat crops told us that the passing of

Regiment Cam

l Mazar.

the desert was at hand. At 1 o'clock the following morning we moved off again. Towards dawn we could feel a difference in our horses' stride, and dismounting more than once in the dark, our feet found firm ground and brushed something—could it be wet grass— that brought back recollection of by-gone days. And daybreak came. The sun rose on the ridges towards Khan Yunus. Clad in the softest green, with the darker sheen of the young wheat crop frequently showing, speckled with the scarlet and yellow of the poppy and anemone, they lay before our dazzled gaze. The lark fluttered skywards from under our hoofs, and the glorious breeze of the spring morning came like a harbinger of peace breathing on paradise, or so it seemed to many men after a year amid the desolations of the Sinai desert.

Moving towards Khan Yunus we became supports to the New Zealand Brigade, which, with a battery of artillery, made a reconnaissance of the village. While the guns thundered out a few rounds we lay on the grassy hillsides above Rafa enjoying the glories of a Palestine spring morning, while our horses cropped the newly-found grass, and (be it whispered) enjoyed many a mouthful of green wheat. Withdrawing later in the day, the Regiment returned to Sheikh Zowaid and established itself in camp on the beach opposite the village. While at this camp, Chaplain-Captain M. R. Maley reported for duty, and was attached to the Regiment. For ten days we remained at Sheikh Zowaid, and on alternate days made strong

reconnaissances in the vicinity of Khan Yunus.
The enemy had gradually withdrawn from the
village and appeared to be holding lightly the
village of Belah, several miles beyond, and his
fortified positions around Weli Sheikh Nuran. A
small force of his cavalry were occasionally
sighted patrolling south and south east of Khan
Yunus, but all attempts to persuade him to a test
of strength proved unavailing.   Gradually we
made good the villages of Khan Yunus and El
Fukharia, up till then No Man's Land; and on
March the 8th we moved to a new camp site
several miles up the beach at Bir Abu Shunnar.

Reconnaissance work continued.   It proved a
welcome change from the similar occupation of
our days in the desert.   In place of ploughing
through endless sand to some hod possibly not
marked on the map, we moved through cultivated
land, among villages, and Bedouin encampments.
The weather remained mild and dry, and the return ride after the longest day, was always over
firm ground and ended at an ocean beach camp.
From Shunnar we patrolled thoroughly the
country to the south of Khan Yunus and El
Fukhari.   Frequently we observed patrols of
enemy cavalry, but all attempts to draw them to a
much-desired trial of strength again failed. They
were not out to fight and small blame to them.
Meantime a large body of our infantry had been
gradually brought up to the front, and the
mounted brigades, resting at various points, were
moved up in readiness for the first attack on Gaza.

The Regiment Bivouacked near Lake Belah.

I

A Patrol Dismounting near El Fukhari

We marched out from Shunnar during the early
morning of March 25th and reaching Deir el
Belah the same afternoon, bivouacked there for
the remainder of the day and subsequent night.
The strength of the Regiment at this period consisted of 22 officers and 426 other ranks. At 3
o'clock on the morning of the 26th we marched
out from Belah as part of the mounted force
whose task it was to envelop and isolate Gaza. By
one of those unlucky strokes of fortune, the whole
enterprise was handicapped by a very heavy fog,
which did not lift till well into the forenoon. The
dash around Gaza was a peculiarly difficult feat,
testing to the utmost powers of leadership and
individual horsemanship. But well before midday we had quietly completed the encircling
movement, and, the Regiment being Brigade reserve, established itself on a series of ridges to
the north-east of Gaza and commanding the main
entrances to the town. Three troops under Major
Cross, and one under Lieut. Hardy, were posted
on positions overlooking the beach and the eastern
road to delay any possible enemy reinforcements
arriving from that direction.

The delay caused by the fog proved fatal to the
frontal attack launched by the infantry. Gallantly
all day they attempted to force the difficult redoubts commanding the southern and eastern
quarters, and they suffered very heavily in attempting to storm positions with the bayonet. The
Turks had chosen their positions well. For miles
to all fronts the gentle slopes were absolutely

coverless. Not one yard of the general advance
could be made, once within range, except under
a hail of shrapnel and withering bursts of machine
gun fire; and even then it was darkness which
robbed the British Infantry of their victory.
Sundown found them hammering hard at the
historic gates of the famous city. But sufficient
support was unavailable to enable them to hold
what they had won, and darkness proved to be the
signal for a general withdrawal.

Meantime the Regiment had during the day
remained in reserve behind Gaza. Towards evening the mounted cordon around the city began to
be threatened by strong bodies of the enemy ap-
proaching from the east and south. It became
apparent that the withdrawal, if withdrawal there
had to be, would be a difficult and hazardous
undertaking. Towards midnight the Brigade
quietly assembled to the east of Gaza, and moving
by a route marked only by our horses' tracks,
began a night march that was as weird as it was
perilous. Wrapped in a continuous dust cloud,
the column to avoid losing touch, moved at that
concertina pace which was ever the bugbear of the
night ride. Galloping desperately through
the dust cloud in the tail end of the column
disappearing ahead, over stony hills and
broken wadis, the only indication of regain-
ing touch was the shock of one's horse being
thrown back on his haunches. Rarely did the dust
cloud lift sufficiently to enable one to see just
exactly who was ahead. Dotted freely over the

country were the dry stone cisterns of the Bedouin, and a few yards outside the edge of the dustcloud meant a probable fatal accident. A wonderful escape was that of Sgt.-Major Stevens. His horse becoming aware of the cistern just too late to shy off it, made an effort to jump the gaping and stone-circled cavity. Failing to quite clear it, the horse slid down tail first, carrying its rider unhurt 12 feet underground. Fortunately the next man to Sgt.-Major Stevens caught a glimpse of something disappearing in the dust, and pulled up to investigate. Stevens was easily assisted out by ropes and bridle reins, but his horse had to be shot and left in the cistern. Quite easily the disappearance of both horse and man might have remained one of the unsolvable problems of the campaign.

Daylight found us crossing the Wadi Ghuzze, and a few hours later we reached Belah. We bivouacked among some very fine wheat crops now out in ear, and remained in the same camp until the following afternoon when we withdrew to the beach and formed camp opposite the lake. Here we remained for nearly three weeks. In turn, we found day and night flank outposts to the south of Khan Yunus, and patrolled the flat country towards Weli Sheikh Nuran. We also took the usual pleasure in preparing for a G.O.C.'s inspection, which, after several false alarms, failed to eventuate. Preparations were being quietly made for another attempt at Gaza, and the Regiment got its share of roadmaking and filling cisterns in the neighbourhood of Tel el Jemmi.

The second battle of Gaza was not long in coming. On the evening of the 16th we moved out from Belah as part of the Divisional Column, and after a painfully slow all-night ride, found ourselves in the neighbourhood of Shellal. Having watered in the wadi we crossed to its opposite banks, and moved out as divisional support in a demonstration towards Hareira. The weather had by now begun to be reminiscent of the desert heat; but this proved to be one of our easy days. We remained in the vicinity of Goz el Gelieb, where a Bedouin cistern afforded a plentiful supply of good water. Withdrawing at sundown we returned to Shellal and bivouacked for the night on the western bank of the Wadi Ghuzze.

The following day we supplied the screen for another demonstration towards Hareira. We came into touch with the enemy's outposts about midday, and his artillery vainly attempted to reach our supports. Withdrawing again at dark, we returned to the wadi, and having fed and watered, stood by ready to move again just after midnight. Moving off at 1.30 a.m. we reached our rendezvous, south of Mendur, by daylight. The second attack on Gaza had been launched that morning (April 19th). As Brigade reserve we remained in the vicinity of Mendur till the early afternoon. Then, receiving orders to report to General Chaytor, we moved up in readiness to go into action if required. Forming up in line of troop column we dismounted and stood by our horses. Just over the skyline the battle raged; it

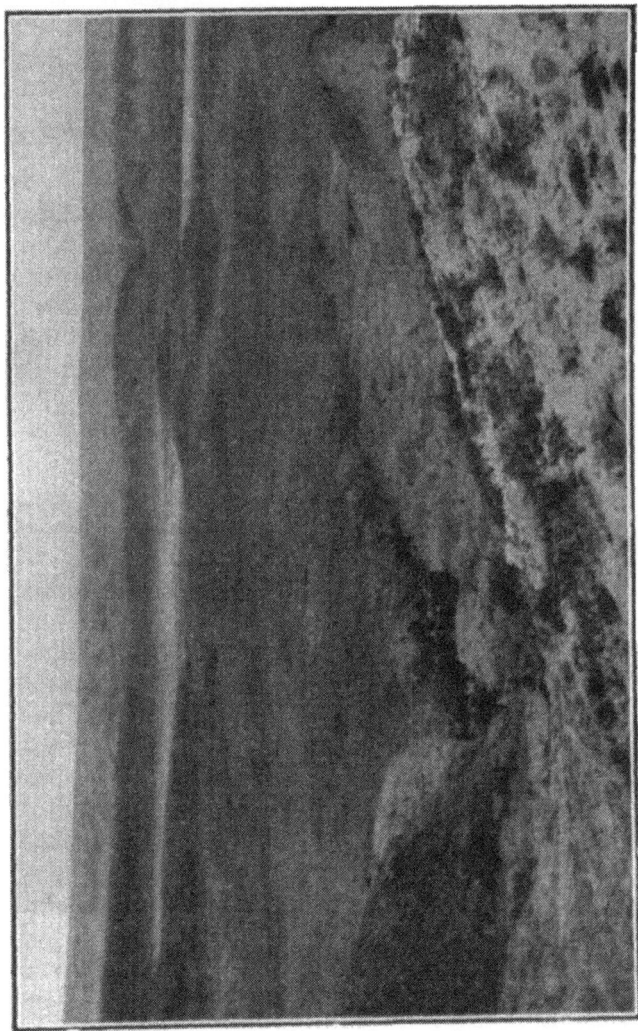

The Wadi Ghuzze near Shellal.

was not long before our turn came to receive the
enemy's attention.   An enemy plane came, saw,
vanished, but ere many minutes passed, it came
again, this time in company with three others.
Kept at a respectful height by our ceaseless rifle
and machine gun fire, they nevertheless spent most
of the afternoon dropping bombs on our area, and
undoubtedly their inaccuracy of aim alone saved
us from a heavy casualty list.   But a battery of
the H.A.C. had been toiling incessantly close to
us during the afternoon, and a thrilling duel resulted with a high explosive gun of the enemy's.
And, later, when we moved off, our medical
limber, mistaken possibly for an ammunition wag-
gon, was blown by the very first shot into match-
wood.   Riding away as we were in line of troop
column in rear of the limbers, the big H.E. passed
directly overhead.   The limber, horses and drivers
had barely disappeared in a cloud of dust and
smoke, when the rarely-failing second shell was
heard coming.   But a number of stretcher-bearers
had already dashed out and were galloping madly
for the medley of timber, iron and mangled men
and horses.   One—Trooper L. R. Henderson, of
C Squadron—timed it to a nicety.   His horse
and the second shell stopped simultaneously, the
latter exploding directly underneath the former.
The horse collapsed in the dense black smoke, and
few expected to see Henderson again except in
pieces.   But a few seconds later he emerged from
the cloud unhurt, and assisted the others in extri-
cating and carrying to safety the wounded limber
drivers.

Withdrawing at dark we moved via Mendur to Heseia, where we bivouacked for the night in support of the outpost line west of the Wadi Ghuzze. The following day patrols left in a southerly and easterly direction. A squadron patrolled to Goz el Geleib, where it engaged a couple of squadrons of enemy cavalry, which, after a brief demonstration, retired towards Hareira, and the squadron returned with half a dozen Turkish ponies and several prisoners. Relieved that evening, the Regiment withdrew to Weli Sheikh Nuran; C Squadron relieved a squadron of the New Zealand Brigade at Tel el Fara. Towering above its banks, Fara was one of the most remarkable landmarks of the Wadi Ghuzze. The Turkish occupants of the previous months had dug a strong redoubt on its summit, and in places the trench revealed the masonry of a many thousand year-old fortification. We now settled down to our usual occupation of holding and safeguarding a flank. Frequently we patrolled to the south and south west of Fara, and in conjunction with other bodies, reconnoitred the No Man's Land between Wadis Ghuzze and Imleh. Finally, by the end of the month, the Regiment, with the rest of the Brigade, consolidated at a point one mile northwest of Fara. We now began to know the playground across the Wadi much as we had known the neighbourhood of Romani. Large digging parties laboured incessantly on roadways across the wadi, and such names and localities as Goz el Gelieb, Karm, Khasif, Goz el Bazal, and different

The Caves at Khaseif.

numbered hills, became as familiar as Katia or Oghritina.

The country which had been green with the just turning crops in the previous month, was fast becoming a dust-heap. We soon found that as far as material discomfort was concerned, the Shellal front vied with the desert in holding the record. The slightest breeze was sufficient to start the dust clouds moving and the twice daily task of watering the horses at the wadi made teeth grit in more than one sense.

On the 18th of May we moved camp to El Sha'uth, which took us a good three miles off the precious Wadi water. Big improvements were being made in the supply. At Shellal, a concrete embankment impounded a miniature lake several feet deep; troughing had been installed at numerous points, and cisterns of drinking water were available at every recognized watering station; but it was largely through their own efforts that the men obtained a supply sufficient for the necessities of health. Few men returned from a watering parade without a bucket on either foot or their section's water-bottles round their necks. And the chronic dust nuisance, combined with the growing summer heat, made the possession of the Wadi Ghuzze water supplies essential to the maintenance of mounted troops on that flank. At Sha'uth we camped in Turkish dug-outs which had been abandoned almost unused.

On the 22nd the Regiment moved out to take part in the demolition of the enemy railway which

ran from Beersheba through Asluj. Crossing the
Wadi at Fara we joined up with the 1st Brigade
early in the afternoon, and proceeded to Bir Esani,
about nine miles up the wadi; arriving there by 6
o'clock.   After a couple of hours' spell we
marched out for Khalasa.   Riding till 2 o'clock
the following morning, we eventually surrounded
and outposted Khalasa, cutting the telegraph line
to Beersheba.   One troop of B Squadron, under
Lieut. MacKenzie, accompanied the 1st Brigade
a further 10 miles to Bir Asluj.   There the demolition of viaducts and the railway line generally
was successfully carried out.   The Regiment spent
the day outposting and patrolling in the vicinity
of Khalasa.   During the afternoon we withdrew
and returned to Esani, and after a "feed up and
boil up" halt, resumed our journey back to
Sha'uth, arriving in camp about midnight.   The
return march was a very trying one.   The night
was particularly hot and devoid of any breeze, and
practically the whole country had become a dust-
heap.   But a welcome relief was at hand.

On the 28th we were relieved, and after a few
hours' ride established ourselves in a soldiers'
paradise, a camp in the soft clean sand at Tel el
Marakeb.   For three precious weeks we rested.
The soft sea air and the rolling surf made Nature's
original idea of nakedness irresistible.   Except
when on duty, clothes were practically discarded,
and before long the beach might have been mistaken for a resort of South Sea Islanders.   The
climate on the Palestine beach was truly magnifi-

Demolition of a Viaduct, Beersheba-Asluj Railway.

K

cent. Hot only for a couple of midday hours, the remainder of the day was fanned gently by the soft warmth of the Mediterranean breeze. After the dust of the arid areas of Sheikh Nuran and Fara, we decided that the cleanliness of the desert sand, still represented in the chain of giant sand-hills fringing the Palestine coast, was something we had never quite given it credit for during the days in Sinai.

Towards the end of June we moved out again, and being now in reserve to the Division, a short ride brought us to a camp site just beyond El Fukhari. Here we remained for a fortnight. Beyond ordinary regimental and brigade duties and the eternal stables and watering parades, life was quiet; but the spectre of never-ending dust haunted both waking and sleeping hours. We found time to meet and defeat the 1st Regiment at football, and after another brief week's camp at Marakeb, we marched out for our last turn in holding the flank positions on the Wadi Ghuzze. Camping close to the wadi banks at Um Urgan, we settled down again to the same round of patrolling No Man's Land, reconnaissances of the enemy's strongholds across the Wadi Imleh and the never-ending work of improving and consolidating the sector.

One noteworthy night's work was the exploration on foot of the enemy's territory across the Wadi Imleh. Leaving camp after dark, the Regiment crossed the neutral ground between the two wadis, and leaving horses concealed under the

steep banks of the Imleh, A Squadron, under
Major H. D. White, proceeded on foot out into
the blue. One troop of C Squadron, under Lieut.
Black, accompanied A Squadron, and remained on
post some distance out overlooking the Beersheba
Road. Cut off practically all night by trains of
Bedouin and Turkish camels, and running the
hourly risk of discovery by patrols of Turkish
cavalry, the night became a supreme test of vigi-
lance and absolute control, under the most trying
circumstances, with the knowledge that the
slightest error would imperil the success of the
squadron reconnoitring further out. Lieut. Black
and Sgt. Ridgway were awarded respectively the
Military Cross and Distinguished Conduct Medal
for their work that night. But by one of those
peculiar coincidences, neither ever wore the ribbon
of his distinction. Lieut. Black was mortally
wounded several weeks later during an outpost
skirmish at Hill 630, and died several days afterwards, the news of his decoration coming through
the day he was wounded; and some nine months
later, the belated news of Sgt. Ridgway's D.C.M.
came to us several days after he had fallen in
action at Amman.

In losing Lieut. Black the Regiment lost one of
its most conscientious and fearless officers. A man
who played the game of soldiering right up to the
hilt; it was over conscientiousness which exposed
him to the ill-fortune of a fluke. In charge of a
day patrol to Hill 630, overlooking the Wadi
Imleh, he had seen a section correctly posted and

returned to the main body of his troop. But a burst of fire from a Turkish post concealed in the wadi made him return to the post. After satisfying himself that all was well, he crawled away down the hillside, and well below the skyline stood up to return to the horses, when an "over" wounded him fatally in the back.

Alternately we supplied front line, support and reserve with the rest of the Brigade. We became case hardened to the never-ending dust, and our closeness to the plentiful water supply of Shellal, made life a good deal easier. The health of the Regiment, beyond the inevitable daily septic parade, remained good, and the horses proved then, as they had been throughout, that for endurance the Australian bred animal has no equal. Still a number of the original 1914 horses remained with us, and it was remarkable how they had gradually narrowed down to a type, the compactly built "big" little horse, which had nearly always proved a good "doer." Finally our last stay on the Shellal front came to a close. Early in August we were again relieved, and marched in once more to Marakeb, settling down to a well-earned enjoyment of rest and surf. The establishment of a Y.M.C.A. and a brigade stadium helped to vary the daily programme of sleep and surf. Once more we decided that Chidley deserved canonization instead of mockery. The month wore away and we spent it storing in a new supply of health and vigour for the big move impending.

During the first seventeen days of September, the Regiment remained in its rest camp at Tel el Marakeb. Instructional work continued, a number of officers and N.C.O.'s attended Vickers' gun classes supervised by the O.C. of the Brigade Machine Gun Squadron, and at D.H.Q. the Divisional Gas Officer lectured to classes of N.C.O.'s. Musketry practices with, and without gas helmets worn, were carried out, and the whole camp area, arms, saddlery and all gear were thoroughly cleared for the Corps Commander's inspection which took place on the 13th inst.

The rest at Marakeb was greatly appreciated by all ranks. The various boxing tournaments and other sports, surfing, sunbathing and the sea breezes heartened up the men a good deal for another turn on the arduous and dusty front of the Wadi Ghuzze.

The Regiment, with a marching out state of 23 officers, 438 other ranks, and 565 horses, left Marakeb on the morning of the 18th inst., and after two hours' ride reached its new camp at El Kazar, taking over the site previously occupied by the 9th L.H. Regiment. Being in supports here, instructional work continued, gas drill, Hotchkiss and rifle practice and tactical schemes being the chief features. The regimental lines were inspected on the 28th inst. by the Commander-in-Chief.

The first three weeks of October were uneventful. Ordinary camp routine and instructional work, similar to that of the previous month, continued. The dust nuisance was very great, owing to the prevailing wind being invariably from a certain quarter, horses going to water had to move in a continuous dust cloud both ways.

On the 8th October we enjoyed the spectacle of a thrilling air fight in which the enemy plane was finally brought down, crashing across the Wadi Ghuzze at Goz el Basal.

During a divisional presentation of medals by the Commander-in-Chief, R.S.M. Hanton and Sgt. Macansh were decorated with the Servian Star and the D.C.M. respectively, and on the 18th inst. Lt.-Col. Fuller left for Australia on four weeks' furlough.

On the 21st inst. the Regiment moved out of camp and having joined up with the Brigade, left at 5.30 p.m. for Esani, 14 miles distant, and arriving there at 10 o'clock, bivouacked for the night. During the march C Squadron provided the left flank and rear guards. Next morning the camp was moved three miles up the wadi, and during a stay there of three days we provided working parties and various patrols and outposts.

On the 24th inst., the Regiment joined up with the rest of the Brigade and moved to Bir Asluj, a distance of 17 miles S.E. of Esani, arriving there at 1.30 a.m., bivouacking and outposting for the remainder of the night. Major H. D. White took command of the Regiment as Temporary Lt.-Col., vice Lt.-Col. Fuller on furlough, and Sergeants Crane and Sharpley were granted commissions.

For five days the Regiment remained at Asluj cleaning out wells which had been blown in by the enemy. This work proceeded in shifts day and night and was undoubtedly one of the most arduous undertakings the Regiment ever accomplished. The water supply available was so small that a large number of horses had to be sent back to Khalasa. In addition we found day patrols to various points and night outposts around the camp area.

On the night of the 30th, the Regiment moved out to take its part in the flanking movement around Beersheba. The country travelled over was very difficult, hilly and stony, but by daylight the flanking movement was complete. Reconnaissance was carried out towards Sakaty, and that night outpost positions were taken up astride the Beersheba-Hebron Road. The water supply in this locality was almost non-existent, save for a few Bedouin underground reservoirs and a scanty surface supply in the wadis, the latter due to a providential storm a few days previously.

On the 2nd November the Regiment moved out along the Hebron Road to the Dhaheriyeh Hills, and were held up by strong forces of the enemy and by snipers in impregnable spots about 12 miles from Beersheba.. Till the 6th inst. a very unequal warfare continued in rough country, the difficulty of water supply for both horses and men, the heat by day, and the continuous night outpost work, was very trying to all ranks.

The Dhaheriyeh Hills will remain in the

Temp. Lt.-Col. H. D. White, D.S.O., who Commanded the Regiment from November, 1917, to March, 1918.

Watering Horses at a deep well on the Beersheba-Hebron Road.

memory of the Regiment as one of the worst spots it ever campaigned in. The number of casualties was not great but its personnel was sorely missed. C Squadron, in losing Captain A. C. Thompson and Sergeant R. J. Foster, M.M., suffered an irreplaceable loss. Enemy snipers in this locality commanded great respect, both Captain Thompson and Sergeant Foster being among their victims.

The case of Sergeant Foster was particularly hard. He was one of the early 1914 enlistments, and up till the time of his death he had been off the strength of the Regiment for 14 days only, due to light wounds received at Romani. On completion of his three years' service, which included 30 weeks on Gallipoli without being off duty a single day, Sergeant Foster, a married man with two children, applied for furlough on family reasons. His application for leave was refused on the grounds of insufficient reinforcements from Australia, while the genuineness of his case was admitted. Now his gravestone stands in the cemetery at Beersheba, far from his New England home, and remains one—and not the only one—of the monuments to the selfish cowardice of a large number of his countrymen.

Just prior to the 6th inst. Lance-Sergeant F. L. Ridgway and S.Q.M.S. A. B. Campbell were granted commissions.

On the 6th inst. the Regiment, less two troops left behind on observation posts under Lieut. Hardy, withdrew from its position to within two

miles of Beersheba. The same afternoon a move
was made in a northerly direction and after travelling practically all night and next morning we
camped at Kh. Umn Ameidat, near the Turkish
railway line. The following day, the 8th inst.,
the Regiment moved in support of the 5th, and
working round on their left engaged part of the
retreating Turkish force, capturing a field piece
with limbers and ammunition. During the day
Lieut. H. Dickson was wounded and Sgt. Barrow
killed. The Regiment bivouacked for the night
near the Reservoir at Jammameh. Next day, the
9th inst., the whole Brigade moved in pursuit of
the retreating Turkish Infantry. The Regiment
became engaged with the enemy at Beit Affe,
capturing two guns and co-operating with the 7th
Regiment on our left.

During the Beersheba operations and ensuing
advance towards Jaffa, the great advantage of
mounted mobility was strikingly demonstrated
again and again, but never more so than by the
flanking movement carried out by the 6th Regiment at Beit Affee on the 9th November. For
several days the Turkish Infantry, driven from its
strongholds on the Gaza-Beersheba line of defence, was gradually retreating northwards, taking
every advantage of the hilly formation of the
country to hold up the constant pressure of the
mounted troops in rear. For two days the 6th
Regiment had been taking part in this pressure,
and at Beit Affe on the 9th inst. seized a unique
opportunity of proving how a retreating and de-

feated army is at the mercy of a mobile mounted force, directed by a cool and resourceful brain.

Moving out from Kh. Jammameh on the morning of the 9th, the 6th Regiment at midday sighted a body of about a thousand Turkish Infantry two miles to the N.W. in full retreat. Co-operating with the 7th Regiment on its left the pursuit was at once begun. The formation of the country, hills running at right angles to the line of advance, greatly assisted the enemy in fighting a stubborn rearguard action. Flanking tactics, alternately to the right and left, carried out with daring disregard of the enemy's rifle fire and at full gallop, forced him to abandon in turn one position for another, two striking phases of the drive being the practical immunity of the extended and galloping horsemen from the enemy's rifle fire and machine gun fire, and the extreme speed with which the enemy evacuated one position after another.

The drive continued the whole afternoon, extending over a depth of ten miles, and finally about 5 o'clock the enemy were driven from the hills and took up a strong postion in the Wadi Ghuet, a deep waterway traversing flat and coverless country on which a frontal attack was impossible. One squadron of the Regiment moving at the gallop, immediately proceeded across the enemy's front to some low ridges on the right flank whence the Wadi Ghuet, distant half a mile, could be more or less subject to enfilade fire.

The enemy at once attempted to move from its position, but the flat coverless nature of the ground placed it at the mercy of our rifle and machine gun fire, and those who survived the attempt immediately retired to their position in the wadi. Meanwhile the remainder of the Regiment moved to the same flank and by shifting ground to a position about a mile south of Hill 194, while still covering the country to the rear of the Wadi Ghuet by rifle and machine gun fire, made any further retreat impossible.

A troop on patrol was immediately despatched completely to clear the ground in rear of the Wadi Ghuet. Similar tactics had been carried on all day by units working on the left flank, with the result that, with a few exceptions, who escaped during the darkness of the night, the whole of the Turkish force, which for ten miles had been harried and flanked were glad to surrender to the 7th Regiment. Our casualties during the day were four wounded, due to the speed with which the Regiment moved, and the unerring judgment of troop and squadron leaders in selecting positions of advantage. The enemy's losses were severe, 50 killed being counted in the Wadi Ghuet. Both pursued and pursuers were similarly armed; neither side had the assistance of artillery, but the outstanding advantage of mounted mobility made all the difference in the day's drive, to our light number of casualties, as well as to the final result.

The water difficulty had, since departing from Beersheba, been very severe, all the horses had been without for 60 hours and some for 72. Wells had been discovered in villages, but mostly at too great a depth to allow for quick watering; a necessity in view of the fact that many of the wells were under enemy observation and artillery fire.

For several days the pursuit continued, the Regiment finally moving on to the beach at Hammame for a two days' rest. Here the two troops left under Lieut. Hardy on the Hebron Road rejoined us.

On the 12th inst. the Regiment moved eastward and then northward by Kezazeh, El Kubeide and Ramleh to two miles N.E. of Ludd.

For several days we carried out patrol and reconnaissance work around Wilhelma and towards Ras el Ain and Mejdel Yaba.

During one morning on which C Squadron was on patrol, the enemy heavily shelled and attacked Wilhelma, then occupied by Imperial troops. One troop of C Squadron, while withdrawing from range of snipers' fire, became aware of an enemy movement attempting to flank the railway line east of Wilhelma. The N.C.O. in charge, Sgt. J. M. Bargh, immediately galloped his troop into position near the railway station, and from a cutting completely held up the Turkish advance with rifle and Hotchkiss fire, thus preventing the probable flanking of the village and its capture. This gallant conduct won him the D.C.M. decoration.

On the 26th inst. the Regiment moved on towards the front line beyond Jaffa, and eventually took over part of the outpost line, which consisted

L

here of a series of small redoubts on ridges surrounded by a large orchard of almond trees.
Large digging parties were found every night, and
on the 29th inst, two troops of A Squadron, to co-
operate with the I.C.C. in an attack on point 265,
moved forward on a bombing raid on the enemy
post immediately in front of the salient.   They
drew very heavy rifle and machine gun fire, and
eventually were driven back to their supports by a
strong enemy counter attack.   Lieut. Ronald was
badly wounded, and two other ranks were killed
and two wounded.

During the month the following decorations
were awarded:—Lieut. H. Dickson, the Military
Cross, and Sergeants Potter and Sheridan,
Troopers Smith, McNamee and Hindmarsh, the
Military Medal.

The month of December opened with the Regiment still holding redoubts in the almond orchard
around One-tree Hill.   The horses had, meanwhile, been sent back towards Selmeh village for
safety from shell fire, and on the night of the 1st,
the Regiment was relieved by the 5th L.H., and
withdrew into reserve about half a mile behind the
firing-line.

The enemy had been observed digging in on the
salient in front of One-tree Hill.   A raiding party
from C Squadron, comprising 5 officers and 100
other ranks, Captain D. C. Close in command,
was detailed to attack the salient, the principal
object being to discover whether the enemy were
intending to fortify and permanently occupy this
point or not.

The scheme of attack was as follows:—The raiding party took up a position in the orchard in front of the One-tree Hill post, covered by an artillery barrage which after 10 minutes firing had orders to lift for 10 minutes and then again concentrate on the salient. During the 10 minutes following the lifting of the barrage the party was to rush the salient, scupper its occupants, determine the nature of the enemy's position, and retire on the forward post at One-tree Hill. But owing to inaccuracy of aim, or a defective gun, the whole of the raiding party came under heavy shell fire during the 10 minutes barrage. In that short space of time 23 casualties occurred, yet the only men who moved from their ground, were the stretcher bearers, whose work that night well earned a decoration for every man. No severer test was ever put on a squadron of the Regiment, and in spite of its heavy loss, the raiding party rushed its objective as soon as the barrage lifted, bayoneted 20 of the enemy, and returned to One-tree Hill bringing a number of enemy rifles, four prisoners, some of our own wounded, and the required information regarding the enemy's position.

The squadron's total casualties during the raid were one officer (Lieut. Owen Tooth) and one other rank killed, and one officer (Lieut. N. Dickson) and 22 other ranks wounded.

On the 6th inst. the 2nd Brigade was relieved by an Infantry Brigade in the front line, and that night moved back to Ayun Kara, near Richon. Rain set in during the night and continued inter-

mittently for the next two days.   On the 12th
inst. the Regiment moved, with the rest of the
Brigade, to Esdud, and for the remainder of the
month carried on usual camp routine, instructional
work in gas drill, musketry and Hotchkiss gun-
nery.

For work done during the salient raids, Sgts.
McNair and Baird, Corpl. Capel, and Stretcher-
bearer Bassett were awarded the Military Medal.
Lieut. Ronald also received the Military Cross.

On the 14th inst. one officer (Lieut. H. Dickson) and seven other ranks were presented with
their decorations by the Divisional Commander,
and on the same day three N.C.O.'s (S.S.M.
Stevens, Sgt. Berrie and Corpl. Busby) left for
the Cadet Course at the School of Instruction,
Zeitoun.

The New Year opened with showery weather.
On the 12th inst the Regiment moved out with the
Brigade and proceeded to a new camp at Wadi
Hanein.   Rain fell throughout the day, night and
following day.

The month as a whole was uneventful. Various
branches of training were continued with, and
officers and men availed themselves of leave
granted to Port Said and Alexandria.   Major
Ferguson and Lieut. Marks were transferred to
the 2nd L.H. Training Regiment at Moascar, and
Major O'Brien returned to the Regiment for duty.
Lieuts. W. J. Weir and A. W. Farquhar were
transferred to the Australian Flying Corps as
observers.

During both January and February the weather
continued very inclement; cold, rainy and windy.
The monotony of training and the weather was
varied to a certain extent by a Divisional Football
Competition.   In February, Lieut. Crane was
attached to the Cadre at Moascar.   Lieut. Phillips
left for a months' leave to Australia.   Lieut.
Hewetson rejoined the Regiment from duty on
railway construction, for a week, and then returned
to detached duty.   Lieut. A. B. Campbell was
taken on the strength from Moascar.   The
Divisional Football Competition was concluded,
by the Auckland Mounted Rifles team beating the
6th Regiment in the final by 6 to nil.

A number of officers attended school during the
month: Lieuts. Sharpley and Campbell the Junior
Officers' School at Kelab, Lieut. Allman a Hotchkiss course at Zeitoun, and Lieut. Ridgway reported back from the Cavalry course.

The first two weeks of March were uneventful.
On the 9th inst. Lieut. H. Dickson and an N.C.O.
were sent on a special duty to Jericho, the first
move made by the Regiment .towards the Jordan
Valley.   On March 13th we marched out with
the Brigade and proceeded to Latron en route for
Jerusalem.

The three days' camp at Latron will be long
remembered by the Regiment.   Rain fell almost
unceasingly, bitterly cold winds prevailed, and mud
rendered the camp almost uninhabitable.   On the
17th inst. Latron was left behind and the long
ascent up the Judean Hills to Jerusalem was com-

pleted by nightfall.   The Regiment bivouacked
outside the N.W. corner of the walls of the old
city.   Parties in turn were to visit the historic
places in the old city, then rather in an insanitary
condition, its occupation by our forces having not
been sufficiently long to work the vast improvement noticeable a few months later.

CHAPTER VI

AMMAN AND ES SALT

ON the 22nd inst. the Regiment moved out
again and began the long descent into the
Jordan Valley. During a three days' halt,
just beyond Talaat ed Dumm, Lieut.-Col. Fuller
rejoined the Regiment from his Australian leave,
Lieut. Campbell from hospital, and 2nd Lieuts.
Berrie and Stevens from the Cadet School,
Zeitoun.

From Talaat ed Dumm glimpses could be obtained of the Jordan Valley, the Dead Sea, and the
frowning ramparts fringing the Land of Moab.

Since crossing the Suez Canal, the blue line of
the Judean mountains had always arrested the eye;
speculation as to what lay on the other side of that
blue line, always looming like a will-o'-the-wisp on
the horizon, had been rife since the early days in
Sinai. Now at last the divide had been crossed,
and the night ride down into the Jordan Valley,
and the crossing of the historic river at daybreak,
were the culminating points to the long weary
months in the desert, the waterless, trackless day
and night patrols, and the subsequent sequel to
historic Romani, the gradual pushing of Turkey
from the sacred spots of antiquity.

Daylight found us traversing the eastern plain
of the Valley. Traces of the previous day's con-

flict when the crossing of the river had been forced by the New Zealand Brigade were noticeable in enemy dead and wounded.

The route taken passed through a magnificent wheat crop, irrigated by water drawn from the perennial wadis at the junction of plain and foot-hills. The first objective, Tel el Muslim, was attained without serious opposition, a forward move was made to get into touch with large bodies of enemy horsemen observed on ridges four miles to the south. The enemy withdrew as we advanced, and by four o'clock the ascent of the Moab Mountains had commenced. Rough as they had appeared from the western foothills, the reality far transcended the worst estimate. The ascent, during a night of rain and pitch darkness, in single file by what were goat tracks, along sheer descents, up steep grades made slippery by wet flagstones, was accomplished by daylight, and without one serious accident; a striking proof of the claim that in no phase of the Sinai-Palestine Campaign, were Australian horsemen and their camel transports unable to take part.

The achievement of the camel transport in supplying practically full rations during the whole of the Amman campaign, over the worst country and over rain sodden soil, was unparalleled, and if ever devotion to duty was conspicuous, the officers, N.C.O.'s and Gyppo drivers of the C.T.C. exhibited it to the highest degree.

By four o'clock the Regiment had reached a spot three miles east of the village of Naaur,

Between Talaat-ed-Dum and the Jordan Valley.

The Brigade halted during Amman Operations, March, 1918.

where it remained all day, finding outposts on the surrounding ridges. The rain, which had been falling intermittently during the night, set in steadily at daylight and continued to fall in torrents during most of the day. Except on the stony tops of the ridges, the ground, roads included, became a quagmire, and the night march which followed will long be remembered.

Further rain and icy winds chilled the already soaked and weary men to the bone, and the waterlogged soil necessitated standing up during the brief and usually precious dismounted halts. The route followed took the Regiment through Naaur and northward along the Es Salt Road, thence branching off this on to a track leading to Amman. El Fuheis was reached by 7 o'clock where we bivouacked and outposted for the day. Patrols sent out towards the village of Suiveilah brought back 61 Turkish prisoners.

On the morning of the 27th inst. the Regiment moved with the Brigade towards Amman and came into contact with the enemy N.W. of the village by 10.30.

B Squadron, working on the left flank of the 7th Regiment, moved a considerable distance towards Amman, and the remainder of the Regiment, supported by the Machine Gun Squadron, made a direct attack on enemy sangars a little to the right of the village. Further to the right flank a battalion of the Imperial Camel Corps and the New Zealand Brigade attempted an enveloping movement. C Squadron bore the brunt of the regimental attack that day. Dismounting and leaving its horses behind a high stony hill, the Squadron advanced in skirmishing order down a long slope, the only cover being low ledges of rock at long intervals. During the whole of the advance, enemy shrapnel and machine gun fire were delivered in full force. Absence of artillery on our side placed the advancing force at a great disadvantage. Casualties commenced immediately the first ridge was crossed, and though the advance was made with characteristic bravery, the fight was too unequal, and only the opportune fire of one of our machine gun troops from a stone hut on the left flank averted a disaster. The advance continued to within a few hundred yards of the enemy position. By this time the heavy percentage of casualties had so told on the strength of the attackers that a withdrawal was inevitable, and here again the machine guns' covering fire enabled our men to retire to the original starting point, carrying all wounded and most of the killed.

Amongst the killed that day the Regiment lost one of its best soldiers, "Snowy" Collins. A transport driver, when the Regiment embarked for Gallipoli, he was compelled to remain behind when the first move was made from Maadi; nevertheless, when the *Lutzow* was safely out at sea, Collins appeared from somewhere. Allowed to remain with his unit after landing on Gallipoli, he carried on during the ensuing seven months, save for a few days when wounded by a bomb splinter at Lone Pine, and up till a week before the final evacuation, when a second bomb wound in the leg sent him to hospital. Again, a few days before Romani, he was wounded a third time, this time seriously in the back by a bullet which burst after entering. No one expected to see Collins back again; nevertheless, he returned despite a stiff back which could have got him his discharge any day. Throughout the ensuing two years, Collins' name throughout the Brigade became synonymous with cool courage and careless disregard of personal safety. No one can go on for ever. He was instantly killed while working his Hotchkiss gun, after three years and six months' service, and amongst all ranks it is safe to say that no man was more genuinely regretted or harder to replace.

The enemy still held his main positions around Amman, and along the railway line to the north, having heavily reinforced his numbers during the two preceding days.

On the 28th inst., a day for ever historic in the 6th Regiment, a general attack took place. Infantry reinforcements, which had come up the previous day from Es Salt, advanced in the centre, the 7th Regiment on their left, and on their left again, B and A Squadrons of the 6th in that order. A deep, and in places, precipitous wadi ran circuitously through Amman and the different Turkish positions. On the farther side their artillery concealed in gullies, and in some instances boldly in the open, shelled unceasingly as soon as the

attack commenced. Each ridge-top was fortified
by a stone sangar from which a remorseless
machine gun fire played on the attackers. Steadily
the advance continued until finally it reached the
top of a high bare hill overlooking a series of
strong enemy sangars several hundred yards in
front and surmounting rough points just beyond a
gradual and coverless descent. To the right of
the hill, where our advance became arrested by unerring and ceaseless machine gun fire, lay a deep
hollow and again a gradual ascent to a ridge running parallel to a line of advance.

The 7th Regiment was extended from the
bottom of the valley to the ridge on the right; B
Squadron, 58 strong when it started, had spread
out up the steep hillside and along the top to the
left. Major Ryrie had previously become a
casualty, leaving Lieut. H. Dickson in command
of the Squadron. Seeing the strength of the
enemy positions, both to the front and left flank,
he passed a message down to the C.O. of the 7th
Regiment, under whose command he came, that a
further advance was impossible. The reply was
an order for a direct frontal attack, during which
covering fire would be delivered by the post on the
right of the deep valley.

Realizing that an advance was little short of
suicide, Lieut. Dickson three times in all passed the
message down to that effect; on receiving the final
order to advance at all costs, the advance was
made and the cost to the squadron proved staggering. Lieut. Dickson, wounded in the leg just as

Part of the Regiment going into action at Amman, March 28, 1918.

M

the desperate enterprise started, handed his command to Lieut. Ridgway, who with three troops
dashed over the ridge, and under withering
machine gun fire, made an heroic attempt to reach
the Turkish sangar. Lieut. Dickson's estimate of
the impossibility of the task proved only too true.
Of the men who crossed the skyline in the last advance, only one, wounded in four places and with
clothes in ribbons, succeeded in beating the enemy
machine-gunners in a desperate rush back to safety.
Simultaneously with the advance over the top the
remaining troop of B Squadron and the 7th Regiment moved up along the valley and immediately
were met by the same withering cross fire from
several sangars.

The advance was at once stopped; but for the
three troops of B Squadron, which had advanced
at all costs, it was too late. A general retirement
was then ordered. A Turkish counter-advance
followed at once and was sufficiently held up by a
machine gun and two Hotchkiss rifles to allow
those wounded before the final race to death to be
carried safely back. Of the 58 men in B Squadron, 40 were killed, wounded and missing. The
missing included Lieut. Ridgway, Sergeants King,
Burlace and Sharpe, Corporal Redman and 18
other ranks—in all 23.

The officers' casualty list in the Regiment
during the actions on the 27th and 28th was heavy.
Majors Cross and Ryrie, Lieuts. Evans, Lomax,
Campbell and H. Dickson were wounded, and

Lieut. Ridgway missing; the latter eventually discovered to have been killed in action.

The total casualties in the Regiment during the
two days was between 90 and 100.   During the
29th and 30th the Regiment held with a very thin
line the ridges around its bivouac areas.   Two
very striking spectacles were noticed during these
two days.   Horseholders, sole survivors in many
sections, leading the saddled horses of their missing mates, silently echoed the "empty saddle" ap-
peal of Sydney recruiting picnics.   No women here
leading around saddled-up horses though, and no
recruits heartened by Dutch courage, bribed by
insurance policies or conscripted by white feathers,
to fill the empty saddles.

Reinforcements did turn up though during the
day.   A number of armed Bedouins galloped into
the hollow behind the ridges manned to resist an
attempted Turkish advance, dismounted and took
their places in the firing line, a touch of comic
opera in broad contrast to the deadly tragedy of
the two previous days and a biting satire on Australian recruiting methods.

On the last day of March, a general withdrawal
took place towards Es Salt via Suweilah and El
Fuheis.   Rations and forage were drawn at the
latter point, and in driving rain and piercing cold,
the ride to Es Salt began.   By one o'clock in the
morning the bivouac area was reached, and after
a few hours' rest the long descent to the Jordan
Valley by the Es Salt-Jericho Road began.   The

Mount of Temptation.

weather was still bitterly cold and showery; the
downward road to the valley wound round curves
and along gorges following the rushing course of
the Valley of the Nimrin, then a blaze of colour,
the green of the rank growth of herbage plenti-
fully speckled with the scarlet poppy and white
and yellow everlasting. With each mile of descent
the air grew warmer, and for once at least the
Jordan Valley was a welcome sight as the column
gradually drew out of the foothills.

On the 2nd of April the Regiment moved across
the Jordan to a bivouac site on the Wadi Kelt,
near Jericho. For several days we rested, shaking
off gradually the bitter feeling of unrewarded
sacrifices. But ever to the eastern front the grim
and frowning mountains of Moab, rising scarp-
sided and sheer, reminded us of what seemed
almost incredible, that we had ascended them and
fought on the tableland beyond, the stiffest en-
gagements of the Regiment's history, and suffered
irreplaceable losses in officers and men.

On April 11th the Regiment moved to a new
position in the Wadi Aujah, taking over part of
the West Jordan patrol and outpost work.

Daily a patrol reconnoitred the gap between
Musallabeh and the Wadi Mellahah, generally
drawing enemy artillery and rifle fire as it ap-
proached the neighbourhood of the Wadi Bakr.
Another patrol watched the approaches to the
Um esh Shert Ford across the Jordan.

On the 18th inst. the Regiment left its bivouac
area in the Wadi Aujah and moved across the
Jordan early next morning to take part in a
demonstration attack on the Turkish positions on
the eastern foothills.

Shortly after leaving the broken wadi ground,
near the river, we came under heavy shell fire
while crossing at the gallop several miles of flat
and open country in the direction of the Wadi
Kefrein. Again the speed of the horsemen proved
their salvation, only one man during a several
miles gallop being wounded. Finally we took
cover in the Wadi Kefrein. The enemy held the
foothills too strongly to admit of any definite
attack, so our withdrawal commenced. At sundown the Jordan was recrossed and we proceeded
to our former bivouac site at the Wadi Nieumeah,
and on the following day to our old camp in the
Aujah.

Till the 25th inst. we carried on the old routine
of patrol and outpost, and on the 26th moved back
to the Wadi Kelt, crossing the Jordan by the
Ghoraniyeh Bridge and proceeding down the
eastern side of the river to Hadjla Crossing, on
the following day.

For two days we remained there patrolling and
outposting, as usual, and on the afternoon of the
30th the Regiment, less A Squadron, which had
gone on detached duty to the 179th Infantry
Brigade, moved up the river and proceeding along
the Um esh Shert Road finally branched off on to

the No. 7 Es Salt Road, and once again began an arduous night ascent of the Moab Mountains.

By daylight the precipitous passes and rocky defiles of the ascent had been safely negotiated, and we halted for an hour three miles west of Es Salt and fed up. Moving forward again we proceeded along a very difficult track through Es Salt and out on to the Amman Road beyond the town.

In the early afternoon we moved out in the direction of Ain es Sir, reconnoitring some very rugged country. Our advanced guard soon discovered that the enemy held strongly various vantage points around Ain es Sir; so after passing through the village we gradually fell back on to the Amman Road. Here the whole Brigade finally assembled and by midnight had moved back to a point a mile beyond Es Salt on the Shunet Nimrin Road, where we bivouacked till daylight.

During the morning we were attached to the 5th Mounted Brigade, which was holding positions on either side of the Shunet Nimrin Road, several miles from Es Salt towards the Jordan Valley. Dismounted we moved along the road several miles and remained in reserve until 5 p.m., when we took up outpost positions for the night on a precipitous ridge on the left of the road.

Meantime, after dark, the horses had been led down the road to the rear of the outpost lines. Orders had been received to withdraw and report as reserve to the Australian Mounted Division beyond Es Salt, the outposts were withdrawn by

2.30 a.m., and by daylight we had moved back to
Es Salt.

The strain of sleepless nights and strenuous
days of hill climbing was beginning to tell on both
horses and men.   The supply of horsefeed had
been exhausted the previous day, and after a
scanty morning meal no one knew where the next
one was to come from.

At 8.30 that morning (May 3rd) we moved
several miles along the Amman Road to support
three squadrons of the 3rd Brigade, which had
held off for several hours that morning a determined enemy attack, finally capturing over 300
prisoners of the assaulting force.   Remaining in
reserve till midday, we then gradually took over
the 3rd Brigade posts, and when darkness fell a
very thin line in a very precarious position made
its dispositions for the night.   A general withdrawal of our forces was to take place that night,
and the outpost line, extended to very attenuated
limits, was ordered to hang on at all costs, until
instructed to withdraw.

An illustration of the precarious nature of the
position can be found in the fact that one troop of
18 men had to cover 300 yards of front in four
posts.   During the day enemy snipers had been
very active and accurate, and a good deal of shelling at the right of the line had taken place.   To
the extreme left of the position for the last few
hours before the withdrawal, there was no outpost
line at all; had the enemy attempted to flank the

position during the night nothing could have prevented him from cutting the Es Salt-Amman Road behind us.

Fortunately the severe check inflicted on the enemy by the 3rd Brigade that morning had a salutary effect and, except for occasional sniping, the weary outpost line was left undisturbed until two o'clock in the morning, when having received orders to withraw at once, it moved back quietly to its horses, and by half-past three we had passed through Es Salt and reported to B.H.Q. two miles west of the town. The withdrawal to the Valley was continued almost without a halt; we descended again in single file, and generally on foot, the difficult and tortuous No. 7 Road. Finally, with both men and horses nearing the exhaustion stage from loss of sleep, lack of food, severe physical exertion and nerve-racking hours of anxiety, we recrossed the Jordan and bivouacked on the Wadi Kelt a mile from Jericho.

For a week we remained at this camp, and here we were rejoined by A Squadron which had been on detached duty with the 179th Infantry Brigade in the frontal attack on the foothills east of the river.

Till the 10th inst. the Regiment took what rest it could in between the various fatigues, guards and regimental duties. On two successive mornings enemy aeroplanes bombed the Brigade area, no casualties resulting to the Regiment.

A Squadron, during its five days' detached duty, had had an eventful time. During the general infantry assault on El Haud—the main enemy position on the East Jordan foothills—the squadron acted as left flank guard. The march commenced at 7.30 on April 30th, the infantry taking the route via the Wadi Nimrin, with A Squadron, under Major Tooth, in position on the left. Immediately opposite El Haud, and several hundred yards from the initial foothill lay an expanse of thick scrub, and from this point of deployment the infantry advanced on the foothills at two o'clock on the following morning. A Squadron remained behind in the scrub with orders to push on when day broke and make good as much ground as possible astride the Wadis Arseniyet and Abu Tullul.

Patrols were sent out at dawn in the direction of these objectives, but coming under heavy machine gun fire were unable to proceed further than 100 yards from the scrub. Meantime the advance of the infantry had been held up; its forward troops had reached within 300 yards of the summit of El Haud, but when daylight came the position was precarious in the extreme, harassed as they were by heavy fire from either flank, and by artillery fire directed at supports and communications in the rear.

In order to ease pressure, Major Tooth sent one troop, mounted, under Lieut. N. Dickson, to occupy the first line of foothills on the south side of the Wadi Arseniyet. This ground was gained with the loss of one horse only, and it had the effect of forcing the enemy to withdraw his most advanced machine guns from the left. The enemy, by means of fire directed down the wadi, still made the crossing of the Arseniyet impossible. During the day the position remained unchanged, except that the squadron horses had been located and shelled, resulting in the loss of one man and two horses wounded. The whole squadron then took cover at the gallop under the first foothills. An outpost line was formed in conjunction with the infantry and after an intense bombardment, lasting an hour, a general advance took place at midnight. A little ground was gained, and A Squadron was enabled to cross the Wadi Arseniyet, the enemy withdrawing his machine guns which had been commanding that wadi and the Abu Tullul.

The nature of the country; rugged, stony hills and broken wadis, made extensive mounted operations impossible, and the physical efforts required by attackers on foot enormous. During the day two companies of Patiala Infantry were attached to A Squadron, and at 3 p.m. a general attack with El Haud as its objective was launched. Major Tooth had, in the meatime, got into touch with a mountain battery and by directing its fire caused the withdrawal of a machine gun operating from a vital point. Two troops under Lieuts. N. Dickson and Sharpley were despatched up the Wadi Abu Tullul to secure all high ground possible, and reconnoitre the position for the advance. A few Turkish patrols were easily driven in, and the high ground N.W. of El Haud secured. Nevertheless, by means of isolated machine guns and our lack of artillery to deal with them, the enemy prevented any effective flanking movement on our part.

The two troops in the advanced position posted a chain of outposts in the best positions available, and from those spots the whole of the Turkish right flank was visible. Artillery support was applied for, but none was available.

At 3.30 p.m. the Patiala Infantry passed through the outpost lines, moving almost due east in its attempt to take El Haud from the right rear. The enemy had only one gun—a small 77 M.M.—on this flank. His ammunition was practically exhausted, pressure from Es Salt was affecting his morale, and the goal appeared in sight. The Patialas, exhausted by forced march in the heat of the day from Ghoraniyeh and from lack of water, were forced to withdraw by sundown.

During the night A Squadron still held its outpost line, and an advance made by the Patialas up the Wadi Arseniyet was driven back with severe losses.

On the following day after a cavalry reconnaissance which was dispersed with loss by our Hotchkiss and rifle fire, the Turks launched a determined counter-attack against the Patialas, who were then holding the high ground in the vicinity of the Arseniyet. The Patialas were forced to withdraw, although our artillery dispersed the main enemy drive, which was directed down the slopes of the Wadi El Haud. The retirement of the

Patialas left a deep salient in the line, with A
Squadron still holding the extreme left. During
a lull of two hours between enemy attacks, A
Squadron had fortified its position by building a
series of stone sangars several hundred yards in
rear of the front outpost line. The enemy advanced in open formation, preceded by a fringe of
automatic rifles and grenade throwers. Lieut.
Dickson, who had charge of the firing line, as
soon as the enemy attack was launched, had the
horses removed to the rear of the first foothills.
Without artillery support it was impossible to
maintain the advanced positions, so under covering
fire from the reserve troops, the front line was
withdrawn to the prepared positions in the rear.
From this point—the highest in the vicinity—the
enemy's attack was easily held up while daylight
lasted, but with nothing to cover the left—the
whole of the force which had been at Es
Salt having withdrawn—Major Tooth commanded a further withdrawal at dusk to a line
commanding approaches down the Wadi Abu
Tullul; the Patialas covering the Arseniyet and
other wadis on the right of A Squadron.

A general withdrawal took place during the
night, A Squadron forming the rearguard to
the whole force. After the withdrawal had
well started the enemy commenced a general advance down the Nimrin-Es Salt Road and the
slopes of El Haud, but stopped at the foothills,
our forces then being well on the road to the
Jordan River. A Squadron bivouacked on the

Nimrin near Ghoraniyeh, and in the early morning withdrew to the banks of the Jordan below the bridgehead, where both men and horses were given a day's rest, rejoining the Regiment on the morning of the 5th of May. During the whole of the operations, the difficulties of keeping up water and forage were very great. Horses had to be led three miles to water, and everything required on the frontal lines had be packed from near the Ghoraniyeh bridgehead.

CHAPTER VII

THE JORDAN VALLEY

ON the 11th inst. we moved again to the Wadi Aujah, camping in the Wadi Obeideh a short distance from the water. Till the first week in June the Regiment was kept busy. Outpost by night, day patrols to Tell El Truny—a point where the Aujah leaves the western foothills—digging and roadmaking, besides ordinary regimental duties and stables, began to tell on the personnel of the Regiment. The weather now became intensely hot. The men's bivvies and horse-lines had necessarily to be between steep ridges, the air became almost stagnant, and the fly and mosquito, alternately by day and night, spoilt any chance of rest the men did get. One thing stuck to them well: the canteen system was excellent and run on the lines of issue to units on payment. The result was a vast improvement in the daily ration, without which continuous work in the Jordan Valley would have been impossible. Beyond occasional shelling and sniping at the Truny patrol, the enemy remained inactive.

Towards the end of the month Lieuts. Allman and Stevens reported to the Training Regiment at Moascar, and Lieut. Berrie to the Officers' General Course, School of Instruction at Zeitoun.

On the evening of the 5th of June, the Regi-

ment marched out en route for Solomon's Pools,
arriving about midnight at Talaat ed Dumm,
where we bivouacked and remained during the
following day. Moving on again the same evening, we passed through Jerusalem at 2 a.m., finally
reaching our bivouac site beyond Solomon's Pools
by 5 o'clock. The relief from the heat, exhausting work, and insect pests of the Valley, was
almost overwhelming, but the brief fortnight's
rest ended all too soon, and on the 21st the Regiment moved back through Jerusalem, bivouacked
a day at Talaat ed Dumm, and by the 23rd had
taken over a section of the front line on the east
bank of the Wadi Mellahah.

The horses, under the command of Lieut.
Hardy, were sent back into the Wadi Aujah. The
line of defences along the Mellahah consisted of
a series of redoubts on either side. Continuous
work of improvement and consolidation was
carried on. Generally speaking, the enemy was
inactive; a half-hearted raid was made on Tea
Post, but the raiders retired after throwing a few
hand grenades and firing a few rounds. At the
same time a battery threw shrapnel into Tool Post
without doing any damage, and searched at intervals, heavily, the back area towards the Aujah.
The end of June found us still holding our Mellahah positions, any further enemy activity being
directed towards Musallabeh and Maskerah.

The great heat still continued in all its intensity.
The Mellahah position will long be remembered
as one of the worst the Regiment ever occupied.

Watering Horses at the Mellahah-Aujah Junction.

Water was supplied by carts from the Aujah Junction, but the supply never equalled the demand, accentuated as it was by the never-ending heat and the clouds of white dust caused by the lightest breath of air.

On the 3rd of July, the Regiment was relieved by the 7th and returned to the Aujah as reserve unit to the Brigade.

As Reserve Regiment we found the duties more arduous than when holding the line in the Mellahah, but the unlimited supply of water obtainable more than compensated for the difference. Digging and wiring parties had to be found every night, and outpost for artillery protection, and the famous Gap Patrol in addition.

The Gap Patrol involved the protection, first by patrol, and then Cossack post, of a couple of miles of flat country, scrubby and swampy in places, between El Maskerah and the forward positions on the Mellahah. After patrolling the whole distance and dropping Cossack posts at certain intervals, the remainder of the troop took up a support position with a Hotchkiss gun in rear of the line, and everyone endured, as best he could, the incessant mosquito attacks till the withdrawal at daylight. In the water areas under our control the mosquito had been practically exterminated. No Man's Land could not be touched, and despite mosquito netting, a large number of the men who contracted malaria became infected during some night in the Gap.

During the first week of July, 2nd Lieuts. Capel, Halloran and Macansh reported back from the Cadet Course, Zeitoun, Lieut. H. G. Lomax from leave ex hospital, and Lieut. Berrie from the Officers' Course at Zeitoun. Major H. D. White, temporarily attached to the Instructional Staff, and Lieut. Macansh reported to a School at Richon; Lieut. Crane returning from an Officer's Course there.

Lieut. Holt Hardy had a few days previously reported to Moascar for duty, and his subsequent admission to hospital was his first break from continuous service since the formation of the Regiment. Invalided soon afterwards to Australia, he left a gap in C Squadron, and no less in the whole Regiment, which was practically unfillable, and the news of his Captaincy and Military Cross was received with extreme pleasure by all ranks.

On the 13th inst. the enemy began shelling Musallabeh at 5 o'clock; the firing being very heavy just before dark. During the night the long-distance gun, concealed somewhere in the reaches of the Nimrin, shelled the Jericho plain intermittently. At 2.30 next morning the whole of the line was subjected to an intense artillery bombardment and a strong attack launched against Musallabeh and the posts held by the 3rd Regiment. We stood to, ready to be called out at daylight, but the attack proved a total failure, so our assistance was not required. Major D. G. Cross reported back that afternoon from the Rest Camp, Port Said.

On the following day the enemy artillery shelled our back areas a good deal, several shells falling close to B.H.Q., also to the dump and the Wadi Obeideh crossing, causing several casualties. A heavy bombardment of Musallabeh and the Aujah back areas followed, lasting for half-an-hour.

On the 16th the bombardment was continued. Two transport drivers were wounded near the dump, and half a dozen shells fell in A Squadron lines, fortunately doing no damage. The same day the Regiment's tour of duty as reserve to the Brigade ended, and we returned to our old positions on the Mellahah line, A and C Squadrons occupying the posts known as Salt, Safe, Star, Shell and Scrap, with B Squadron in reserve.

Again the weary round of day observation and night outpost, digging and wiring parties continued; heat, thirst and dust by day, and mosquitoes by night making the life of the Askari unbearable to the breaking-point.

Relief came on the 29th inst., when the position was taken over by a Yeomanry Brigade. The Regiment bivouacked a day at the Auja-Mellahah Junction, marching out again that evening, and arriving at Talaat ed Dumm early the following morning. We remained at Talaat ed Dumm for nine days, and then moved on through Jerusalem and Bethlehem to a bivouac site at Beit Ammar, several miles south of Solomon's Pools. The difference in climate between Solomon's Pools and the Valley was almost unimagin-

able. Horses had to be rugged, and instead of
sleepless and sweltering nights, extra blankets and
overcoats were needed. Supplies of vegetables,
tomatoes and grapes were available, and for
another precious fortnight all ranks breathed
again.

DESCENDING INTO HELL

The Bushman had been on duty in Jerusalem.
For two days he had been replacing the dead dust
in his lungs with the sweet clear air of the Judean
mountains. The monotony of the front line fare
had been varied by the delicious grapes and
tomatoes of the upper world, and the absence of
that poisonous heat from his veins almost in-
duced a shiver.

But the job was over, and he stood on the hotel
corner waiting for the first of the endless line of
motor-lorries which started at an early hour every
morning for Jericho. He hopped on to the first
one that came along, one got none of the dust
which came to the middle or tail of the transport
column. Through the city, past Gethsemane and
round the Mount of Olives they sped, and a turn
of the road brought into full view the table-land
of Moab and bitter memories of what had
happened there. Past Bethany and down the steep
slopes, round the abrupt curves, the long line of
lorries moved slowly downwards. The hillsides
grew browner, the scanty dry vegetation disappeared altogether and the wilderness, clothed in
its barren array of precipitous cliffs and loose rock,
settled heavily on the Bushman's soul.

Looking back as his lorry started the descent, near Talaat ed Dumm, he felt thankful he had caught the first one. A whitish ribbon, miles long, marked what he could see of the winding road. There was not a breath of wind. The dust merely rose and hung over the narrow track, shrouding out of sight the long line of transport following closely behind.

The Regiment was still camped in the Mellahah, several hours' ride from Jericho, and the Bushman expected a horseholder to meet him at the dump. He wondered if anything special had happened during his four days absence, probably nothing but more malaria. Anyway, they were four days closer to a move somewhere—anywhere but the Mellahah. Fellows often speculated as to what was the original cause of such formations, the 50-feet deep cliffs of soil and the cup-like dead ends. In his present frame of mind he preferred his own theory, that the original bottomless pit was directly under the Mellahah, and that at one time when the inhabitants had tried to dig out, the earth had slid into the pit like the sand in an hour-glass, until the holes had been blocked.

He'd get back an hour or so before sundown, and he could hear the sergeant warning him for the Gap Patrol that night, before he had tied his horse up on the lines. Well, he'd been out of it for four days, and no one could do many Gap Patrols without getting malaria, so one way or another he didn't give himself long. Would the cursed war never end?

Midday came.   The clear air of the up-lands
had completely gone.   The heat became more
stifling with every mile of the descent, and its
sudden upward rush at quick intervals made body
and brain shudder.   At last the lorry turned a
sharp curve and ran down the final slope of the
foothills.

Unrelieved, save by two touches of colour, the
green which enveloped the hideous squalor of
Jericho, and the distant lifeless blue of the Dead
Sea, the Jordan Valley, steeped in the breathless
heat of the forenoon, lay in all its dreadful reality.
The vast expanse of white dust extended from
foothill to foothill.   At intervals a shaded line
marked the precipitous fall of some wadi, and
midway a dip in the ground, surmounted by a
vista of white cliffs, betokened the course of the
river.   As if in mockery of the morning stillness,
dust rose in funnel-like whirlwinds into the very
heavens, and on every side desolation, disease and
death reigned supreme.

*   *   *   *   *   *

Moving on to the front line we went into camp
at the Aujah-Mellahah Junction as Reserve Regiment and remained there till the end of the month.

On the 1st of September we moved to a new
camp site east of the Jordan River, just beyond the
Ghoraniyeh Bridgehead, taking over part of the
patrol and outpost line then held by the 11th
Cavalry Brigade.   Work, both by day and night
here, proved very severe.   Malaria in all its in-

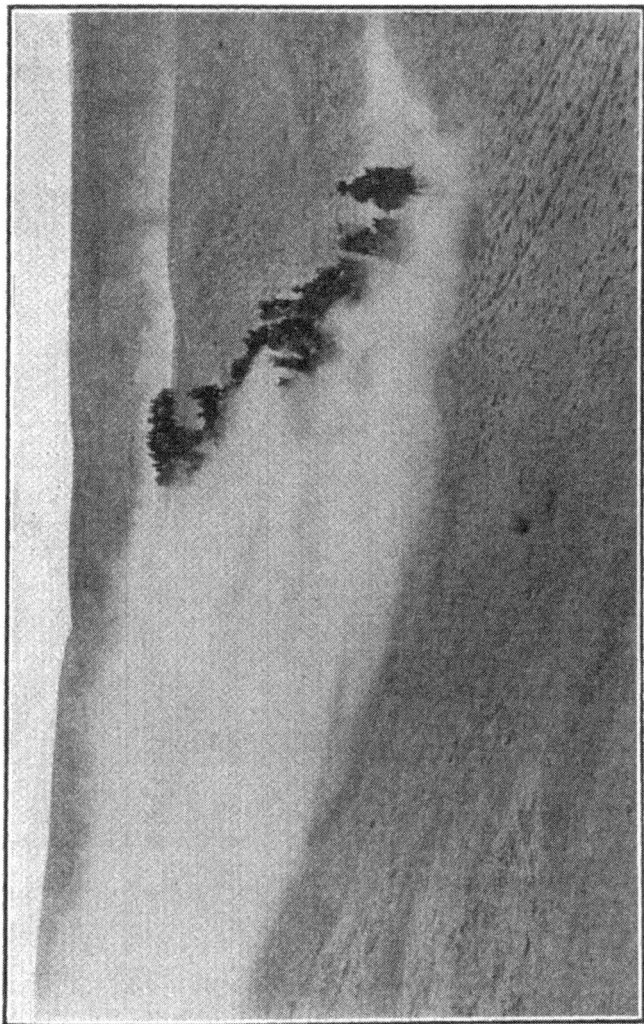

Dust Scene, Jordan Valley.

Dust Scene, Jordan Valley.

tensity had stricken every unit in the Valley, numbers of men were evacuated daily, few reinforcements were forthcoming, and the burden became very heavy on the remaining handful. A daily patrol traversed the country for several miles parallel with the river, and as far east as occasional ambushes by the enemy in patches of thick scrub would allow. One troop of B Squadron was machine-gunned one morning, resulting in one man wounded and missing and two horses wounded. Otherwise the daily and nightly round of duty continued. Occasional Turkish deserters surrendered to the outpost line, and the enemy's long-range gun at intervals shelled the Jericho flats and the Ghoraniyeh Bridgehead.

On the 19th inst., the Regiment received orders to be ready to move at short notice, to take its part in the final destruction of the Turkish Army. Patrols and reconnaissances were specially active.

On the 20th of September, Major Tooth took a strong party along the Arseniyet Road to a point opposite the mouth of the Abuturra Wadi, coming under heavy machine gun and rifle fire. Moving south towards the Nimrin the patrol drew heavy shrapnel fire.

C Squadron, sent out to get into touch with the enemy south of the Nimrin, also came under artillery and machine gun fire, and was followed by shrapnel practically the whole way back to camp. Four horses were killed, and one man, badly wounded, died on his way to the Field Ambulance.

Special patrols were found nightly to a point near the Ghubba Graves to listen for enemy transport moving from Um esh Shert.

For two days the situation remained unchanged, but on the 22nd inst. it became apparent that the enemy was withdrawing. A patrol in the direction of El Haud discovered a deserted cavalry camp in the foothills about a mile and a half north of El Haud.

Proceeding south, and skirting the foothills, the patrol saw no signs of the enemy until Deccan House was sighted, where considerable movement was taking place. Withdrawing the picket post without being fired on, the enemy movement was reported to B.H.Q. and the Regiment received orders to be ready to move at the shortest notice.

At a quarter past 5 on the morning of the 23rd inst., we moved out and proceeded to Khabr Mujahid, reaching there by 7 a.m., and finding the locality clear of the enemy.

Two troops, under Lieuts. Hedley and Lomax, were despatched respectively to Ain Hebussie and Helale. Reporting all clear on these positions, the Helale patrol, supported by another troop, moved to the bridge on the Es Salt-Nimrin Road at Howeij. The Regiment had previously had orders to follow on to Howeij, pick up the patrol there, and then advance by the main road to Es Salt.

The route from Mujahid to Howeij proving impracticable for pack transport, fresh orders were given to advance by the No. 4 Road to Ain

Village of Ain-Es-Sir.

o

Jericho Jane.

Es Sir, with the exception of C Squadron, which, under Major Close, did advanced guard for the 20th Infantry Brigade up the Shunet-Nimrin-Es Salt Road. The remainder of the Regiment reached the village of Sir by 7 o'clock; the No. 4 Road, though still very rough, had been much improved by the enemy since the initial ascent made by us in March. Enemy dumps and freshly-deserted camps on the way up showed that the retiring forces were not far ahead.

The screen, provided by B Squadron, under Major Tooth, passed through Ain Es Sir by 11 o'clock, and on reaching the Cross Roads, drew fire from an enemy 77 M.M. gun from the direction of Sueifiye, one or two shells dropping into Ain Es Sir. After watering horses there, the whole column moved forward, Brigade Headquarters established itself at Ain Eemar, and the rest of the Brigade took up an outpost line from that village to Ain Es Sir, the Regiment's position extending from Ain Es Sir to the ruins on the Naaur-Hemar Road.

On the morning of the 25th, the Brigade moved forward to attack Amman, the Regiment being Brigade Reserve, took up a strong position near Semmak. Very little opposition was encountered, the enemy freely surrendering everywhere.

Major Close had meanwhile reported back with his Squadron. During their advanced guard move up the main Es Salt Road, C Squadron discovered the last resting place of "Jericho Jane," the long-distance gun which made life vivid at

times on the West Jordan flats. The enemy had
attempted to save the gun, but had abandoned it
several miles up the road, overturning it off its
carriage down a steep grade into the Wadi Nimrin. The advance on Amman continued steadily
until within a mile of the village, where it became
held up by machine gun fire. The enemy were
using no artillery, except one small gun, but isolated machine guns in prepared positions proved
very difficult to silence until about 4 p.m. when the
enemy in front of the 5th Regiment suddenly
surrendered. B Squadron, under Major Tooth,
then advanced down the Ain Es Sir-Amman Road
to within half a mile of the entrance of the town,
and drew heavy machine gun fire from an old ruin
on a high ridge north of the town, one man being
killed and two others and several horses wounded.
The machine gun position was immediately rushed
by a detachment from the N.Z. Mounted Rifles,
saving B Squadron from very heavy casualties.

Scattered firing still continued to the north and
north-west, but all opposition to the 5th Regiment
had ceased; its screen, followed by a Squadron, advanced through and established itself in the town.
Everywhere could be found signs of the enemy's
complete demoralization. Small parties of Turks
and Germans were wandering aimlessly about,
surrendering to the first comers; the hospitals were
full of wounded and sick, and filth and insanita-
tion everywhere reigned supreme. After watering
in the main Wadi, the Regiment, less B Squadron,
bivouacked in the centre of the town, opposite the

remains of the ancient Roman Arena. B Squadron was despatched to take up an outpost line towards Ain Es Sir.

On the 26th and 27th the Regiment, having moved to a cleaner camp site a little distance out of the town, got a little rest, which was badly required after the strenuous exertions of the previous few days, capping as they did, the end of the long period of tribulation in the Jordan Valley. The weather, fortunately, was perfect, but the country presented a very different spectacle from the one which met the eye in the early summer, the rank growth of grass and herbage having practically disappeared. Forage now began to get very scarce, patrols were despatched to Naaur and Suweilah on the double task of reconnaissance and foraging, but nothing, except tibbin was obtainable. Two troops of A Squadron, under Lieuts. Britten and Hedley, remained to garrison Ain Es Sir, and on the 28th B Squadron was despatched to reconnoitre the country to Leban, a siding on the Hedjaz Railway, 12 miles south of Amman. Both Leban and El Kastal were found to be unoccupied. Information was obtained from Arabs that a large force of the enemy held Aziza, about four miles from El Kastal, and the Squadron returned to camp via the village of Yadudie.

On the afternoon of the 29th, the Regiment received orders to proceed at once to Aziza, where the entire Turkish force had surrendered to two Squadrons of the 5th Regiment, and assistance was required to prevent strong parties of Arab

marauders from looting the Turkish camp.   The
Regiment made a forced march and reached
Aziza before dark.   Night dispositions were made
in conjunction with the 7th Regiment and the
Turkish remnants, and the bizarre spectacle of a
Turco-Australian outpost line became an accom-
plished fact.

The Turks were in mortal dread of the Arabs,
their outposts continually firing and sending up
flares during the night.   No serious attempts at
raiding took place and at dawn the work of collecting and disarming the prisoners took place.   By
10 o'clock the first batch of 4000 was marched
out, still carrying their arms, to preclude any possi-
bility of a general massacre by Arabs, who were
very numerous, well-armed, and furious at being
baulked of a harvest of blood and loot.

As at Amman, the Turkish positions at Aziza
were in an unspeakably filthy condition, and over-
crowded hospitals were full and sick and wounded.
Considerable enemy war material was collected
and loaded on to a captured train during the day
by the Regiment, and in the evening, having been
relieved by the N.Z. Brigade, we left for Amman,
arriving there at 10 o'clock.

On the 1st of October we received the welcome
news that the Brigade was to move back, en route
for Jerusalem.   Moving out from Amman on the
morning of the 2nd, the Regiment proceeded by
Ain Es Sir and the No. 4 Road to Hadjla, cross-
the river there and going into bivouac near the
monastery two days later.

Aziza Railway Siding.

Regiment Camped near Jerusalem after Final Operations.

On the 7th inst. the Regiment continued its move for Jerusalem; bivouacking on the old site at Talaat ed Dumm for a night, we reached the camp, near the Mount of Olives, on the afternoon of the 8th inst.

During the long ascent from the Jordan Valley many a man cast a backward glance, and many a shuddering recollection of all that it stood for was followed by a feeling of unutterable relief that at last it was all over. Few, very few, of those who went down with the Regiment in March, returned with it in October, and of those few, an infinitesimal number, had defied death and sickness and remained continuously on the ration strength. The reaction proved too great for nearly all. The dread malaria, which many had resolutely fought, proved too much now that the upper air of the Judean Hills had been reached, and numbers collapsed and were evacuated.

The journey back was continued after several days spell at Jerusalem.

On the 12th inst. we left for Wadi Hanein, by Enab and Latron, and after bivouacking a night at the latter place reached our destination the following day.

News of the signing of the Armistice, and the final capitulation of Germany being expected in the near future, nothing was left now but to wait as patiently as possible for the final stage of de-mobilization. A syllabus of training was formu-lated, including drill—mounted and dismounted—preliminary musketry, Hotchkiss practice, bayonet fighting and physical exercises.   Race-meetings, starting with Squadron, and ending with a Divisional, Meeting, proved popular sources of amusements.   Occasional swimming parades took place, and football, in conjunction with other sports, helped the time to pass quickly.

November brought a touch of wintry weather, and on the 7th one officer (Captain F. Marks) and 43 other ranks proceeded by train to Moascar to await embarkation to Australia on 1914 leave. The departure of these 43 other ranks made a big gap in the personnel of the Regiment.   A large majority were tried N.C.O.'s, who had borne for years the brunt of strenuous and continuous service.   The feelings of the remainder, glad to see such service meet its reward, long delayed though it had been, and sorry to lose such comrades, found vent in the vigorous blanketing of all those departing; officers being treated as impartially as anyone else.

On the 11th news was received that Der Tag had arrived, Germany having signed the Armistice.   Beyond the firing of flares and going slightly into liquidation, no special celebrations took place.   Lieut. E. S. Halloran was granted special 1914 leave to Australia and left for Moascar, and on the 15th Lieut. Hanton and five other ranks also departed on similar leave to England. For the remainder of the month sport and training continued, marred only by a considerable amount of rain and cold weather.

The Regiment moving out from Jerusalem for Wadi Hanein.

The Zig-Zag near Enab.

CHAPTER VIII

THE LAST LAP

D ECEMBER opened with an inspection by the Corps Commander, the strength of the Regiment at this stage being 14 officers and 432 other ranks. Training, as in the preceding month, was carried on with. On the 5th inst. Lieut. M. L. Crane departed on 1914 leave to Australia, and a few days later Lieut. Berrie reported back for duty from leave ex hospital.

On the night of the 10th a disturbance took place in the village of Surafend, close to the camp. At a quarter past ten the Regiment stood to, and despatched a mounted patrol to prevent any members of the 2nd Brigade from joining in the disturbance.

The Divisional Race Meeting took place on the 14th inst., and proved a great success, marred only slightly by threatening weather. Lieut.-Colonel Fuller now assumed command of the Brigade, and Major H. D. White, of the Regiment.

The relinquishing by Colonel Fuller of the actual command of the Regiment was received by all ranks with feelings of very genuine regret. Save during his brief furlough in the end of 1917, he had led us since November, 1915, and no leader ever had more thoroughly at heart the interests and welfare of his officers and men. He was always approachable, and always the essence of a sport; no man ever left the orderly room without a fair deal. And the features of his long command of the Regiment in the field, were the unerring accuracy of his always rapid decisions, no less than his actual personal leadership.

Due also to the same leadership was the fact that the Regimental Officers' Mess was, throughout, a happy family. Cliquism was never allowed to raise its head, with the result that no officer of the Regiment was ever as happy as when in his own mess. And right to the end the Colonel's interest in his old Regiment brought him frequently to the lines an always welcome visitor.

On the 17th the Regiment received orders for its final mounted trek to Rafa, and preparatory to the move, conveyed most of its heavy gear to Bir Salem Railway Siding. Heavy rain fell during the afternoon and night of the 17th and during the following morning, right up to the actual moment of moving off. Fortunately the weather fined up then and remained so during the five days' march to Rafa. Major Tooth now assumed temporary command of the Regiment, vice Major White evacuated sick. The march began at 9.15, and via Yebnah, where we made the midday halt, we proceeded to our night bivouac area at Sukirier. The rain had made the black soil portions of the road very heavy, and the transport had considerable difficulty in negotiating them.

On the nights of the 19th, 20th and 21st, we

"The Mascot."

Lieut.-Col. Fuller on "Illawarra."

bivouacked respectively at Mejdel, Gaza and Belah, the latter being the final bivouac camp on mounted trek.

Rafa was reached on the 22nd, a camp laid out and established, but proving too cramped and small an area, a move to a better site a few hundred yards away was made a few days later. On the following day Major D. G. Cross returned from hospital, resuming command of the Regiment, and the old year finally drew to a close, the new one being well ushered in with fireworks, flares and fizz.

Major H. D. White, whose health for a considerable time had been unsatisfactory, was, very shortly after reaching hospital, boarded for Australia. One of the strongest personalities who ever left his mark on a unit, Major White demonstrated most emphatically, during his leadership of the Regiment in the Beersheba operations, his fitness for an even higher command. Given the opportunity, he might have risen to any military height; his leadership of a Brigade would undoubtedly have inscribed another name on a brilliant roll.

The Regiment now entered on a difficult phase of its career, waiting for the final stages of demobilization. The great majority of the oldest and best N.C.O.'s, and a number of senior officers and subalterns had departed on 1914 leave to Australia and England, making the duties of the newly promoted N.C.O.'s a necessary combination of tact and firmness. A syllabus for training was laid down and a Divisional Committee appointed to control all sport, subject to the advice of various sub-committees for each branch. In view of the proposed Military Athletic Gathering in Britain, competitions in football, boxing and pedestrian events were taken in hand. Football in particular, was largely taken up, and a very strenuous competition was inaugurated. None of the Regimental teams competing approached the strength of previous years, the toll of battlefield and 1914 leave affected seriously the old fifteens that played at Hill 70, Hassaniya, Masaid, Abbassan and Wadi Hanein.

The Regimental football had always been at a very high standard. On several occasions we had met New Zealand teams on equal terms, and no other Australian fifteen had ever seriously challenged our claim to possess the best Australian Rugby Union team east of the Canal. But the loss of such players as Hardy, Hedley, Capel, Farquhar and Weir, the two O'Briens, Fenner, Mears, Baird and "Snowy" Lester, made a big difference to any chances we had of winning the Divisional Competition. A few old players still remained, Neil Ross, "Joe" Nevitt, Sedgwick, Reynolds, "Juja" Rock, Fred Walker, "Possum" Gilmour and "Trig" Farquhar, and round this nucleus sufficient newer players rallied still to uphold our previous claim to possess the best Australian team on the front.

The New Zealand Brigade, as usual, put strong and winning teams into the field, the defeat of

A Squadron (Wadi Hanein).

Farewelling a "1914 Leave" Man.

Wellington by Auckland deciding the Competition
in favour of the latter team.

Horseracing again came into much prominence.
A good course was selected, and each unit in turns
did its share towards the necessary appointments.
The Regimental horses, when tried out, furnished
some startling surprises.   Two in particular,
"Sandy" and "Cobar," both in B Troop, B Squadron, deserve immortalization. Both were troopers'
horses since the crossing of the Canal, and
neither had missed a single stunt, drawn an extra
ounce of feed, or carried an ounce less than the
usual trooper's swag from Serapeum to Amman.
In one of the New Zealand Brigade Meetings,
"Sandy," in the Open Mile Handicap, beat the
cracks of the Division, including such horses as
"Illawarra," "Dipso," and the New Zealanders'
"Grey Gown," "Hamaran," "Rototawai," and
"Open Slather," all officers' horses, which in
comparison with "Sandy" had had a time much in
the same ratio to that of their owners.

At a Military Race Meeting, in Cairo, the
Regiment was represented by Lieut.-Colonel
Fuller's "Illawarra," Major Tooth's "Dipso,"
Sergeant Macarthy's "Mazar," and Trooper
Hambly's "Cobar." "Illawarra" won the two-
mile race easily; "Mazar" and "Cobar" fought
to a finish the seven furlong Other Ranks event,
the former just winning, but the rest of the field
hopelessly out of it, and "Dipso" ran a good third
in the mile and a half.

A large number of men attended various classes

and lectures delivered under the demobilization
scheme of education.

During the month the strength of officers in the
Regiment was reinforced by 2nd Lieuts. Busby,
Nevitt and Ross, and the following decorations
were awarded:—Major S. A. Tooth, the D.S.O.,
and Sergeant-Major Sheridan, the D.C.M., two
of the most popular awards ever granted to the
Regiment. Major Tooth's record is worth more
than a passing mention. Leaving Australia as a
Sergeant in 1914, and gradually rising throughout
the various stages of promotion, the name of
Stuart Tooth became synonymous with sterling
work in the field and camp and devotion to duty.
During the whole of the Gallipoli Campaign he
was absent on a fortnight's guard at Imbros only,
and he had the high honour of being the subaltern
chosen to command the final Regimental twelve on
the night of the evacuation. During the whole of
Desert Campaign, from the Canal to Amman,
through the Sinai Desert, the Gaza Front, the
Jordan Valley, and the Moab Mountains, his record was the same, first as troop and then as squadron leader he stuck to his job throughout, and
although a malaria subject for the final six months,
he refused the 1914 leave, preferring to return
with the unit he embarked with.

March opened with warmer weather, the con-
tinuance of the training and educational syllabus.
and a Brigade Race-meeting.

Khamseen weather soon arrived, and for several
days wind, dust and finally showers made con-

" Dipso."

"Cobar."

2

ditions of life very disagreeable, and several parades had to be cancelled.

Leave to the United Kingdom had been granted, and 40 other ranks left on the 5th inst. for Moascar as the Regiment's quota of the 10 per cent. A.I.F. personnel.

Rumours of our speedy departure for home became very insistent, and the departure of part of the 1st Brigade for embarkation pointed to the early dawning of "the day" that by now had excluded everything else from one's thoughts. Horses, saddlery, Hotchkiss rifles, and a large quantity of gear were handed in to various depots, and, save for a few officers' mounts, the camp might have been an infantry one.

The passing of the last of the Regiment's horses might almost be said to be the passing of the Regiment. A small number had been destroyed for reasons of age or debility, but the careful selection in the first instance, and admirable handling by squadron and troop leaders throughout the different campaigns, resulted in a body of horses never excelled and seldom equalled. A considerable number of original 1914 horses saw the campaign through. In the great majority of cases they ran to a certain type, the big "little" horse showing a considerable strain of blood, compact in build, inclined to be nuggety.

Two superstitions our Light Horse campaigns exploded thoroughly. One, the often alleged necessity of a big horse to carry a big man, and the other the unsuitability of a heavy man for mounted work. The latter was disproved many times. It was often noteworthy that during the worst sore-back period—that of Romani and Et Maler—many of the heaviest men left their horses backs untouched. And again, frequently, the big horse caved in under the terrific strain of waterless and foodless periods, and the never-ending desert patrol.

The general efficiency of the Regiment's horse-flesh was largely due to the untiring efforts of the farriers. One and all took their jobs with the utmost seriousness, and the names of such men as Joe Watts, Bill King-horn, Joe McGuinness, Charlie Widstall, Herb. Dew, Frank McCann, Nat Henderson, George Jones and Frank McCormack will always loom large as the *Dei ex machina* behind many a difficult stunt. It is difficult to single out individual horses, as men, but the excellence of our steeds generally was undoubtedly embodied in the Mascot—a thirteen-hand pony. He was presented to the Regiment in 1914, and for a long time re-mained unattached to the ration strength. But eventually he won his right to be regarded as a horse, and throughout the whole of the campaigns carried an average weight man and a full weight of gear. Never did he knock up or cave in, and his fiery disposition was as unquenched when we handed him in in June, 1919, as it was when he em-barked in December, 1914.

It really seemed now that our future movements would be on foot.

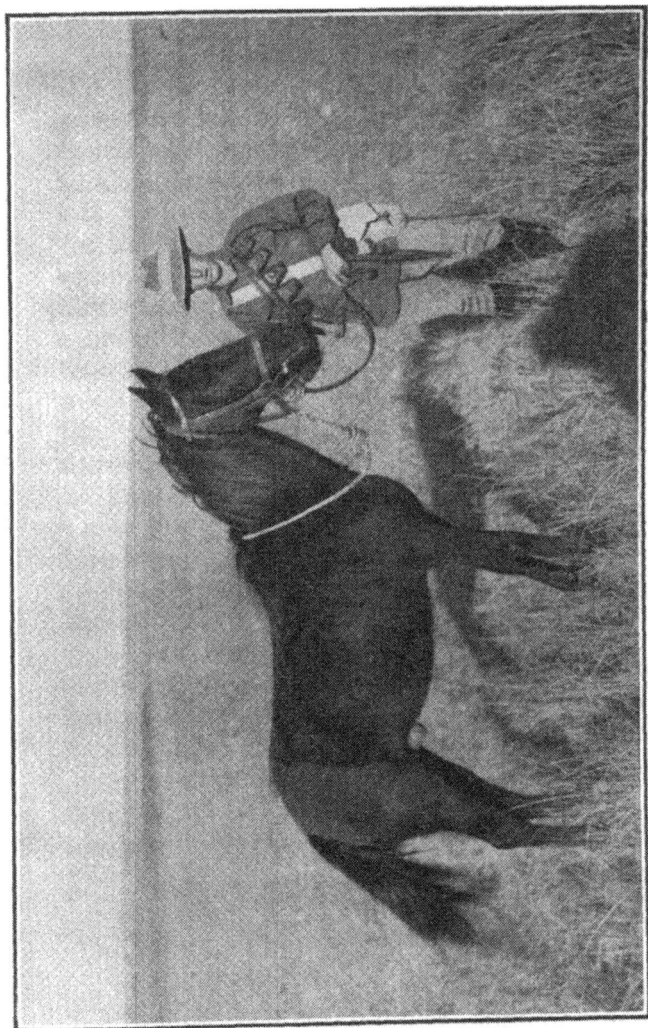

"The Mascot."

But the Regiment was shortly to undergo a disappointment difficult to bear. The riots and general disturbances in Egypt made it imperative to retain all Australian mounted troops available, so almost on the day on which we had hoped to sail, we marched out from Rafa and entrained for Kantara. Camping there for two days we re-equipped. The horses we had handed in—the pick of our best, and our best had never been equalled by any other unit—had been passed on to other Brigades. We had to content ourselves with a mixture of draughts, culls and mules, leavened here and there with a lucky find—by moonlight. Again we moved off, and entraining at Kantara, proceeded to Damanhour, between Cairo and Alexandria. A mile or two outside Damanhour we camped in knee-high berseem, and on every side regrets were expressed that we had not our old horses to let loose in such an equine paradise. For several days we remained in this camp, and then, on the last day of March, entrained again for Quesna, a few miles north of Benra Junction.

During the month the strength of officers was increased by the arrival of 2nd Lieuts. F. C. Lowe and N. S. Reynolds from the Officers' Training Course, Zeitoun.

Our camp at Quesna was in many respects reminiscent of the desert. Several hundred acres of higher sandy ground, as bare as any part of Sinai, formed a marked contrast to the fertile miles of delta country which surrounded it. Regi-

mental Headquarters was established in the house
of an Armenian Loyalist, which stood in an irrigated area of fruit and eucalyptus trees; one green
patch in the sandy waste.   Tents, bivvies and
horse lines were soon erected and again we settled
down to the wearied task of waiting.

Matters had quietened down considerably in
the delta country.   In Cairo and Upper Egypt,
unrest prevailed, but in the districts we were called
on to patrol, everything was peaceful and everyone
friendly—to the outward eye at any rate.

One officer and 50 other ranks were detached
for duty at Quesna Station, where they did police
duty and railway patrols.   Two Squadrons, under
Major Tooth, patrolled a number of villages to
the east of Quesna, and on the 10th April B and
C Squadrons left for the villages of Tala and
Ashmun respectively.   The duties of these detach-
ments were to visit all villages in the locality,
accompanied by a Political Officer, ascertaining
whether proclamations which had been issued and
posted up had been interfered with, and warning
all Sheikhs and Omdahs of their personal responsi-
bility for any damage or disturbance.   At both
villages the Squadrons were hospitably received by
the Mamours (district governors) and during a
week's continuous patrolling, nothing but peace
and agricultural prosperity was encountered.

Both Squadrons returned to Quesna on the 17th
April.

The Wellington Regiment had meanwhile
arrived at Quesna and camped close to us.

Although shorn of most of their glory in the way of racehorses, it was soon decided to give the latest equine recruits a chance to prove themselves, and on the 19th was held the first of a series of race-meetings which did much to alleviate the now almost unbearable feeling of restlessness engendered by the delay in embarkation.

Summer was now fast coming on, but fortunately it proved to be remarkable for lower temperatures than usual. The ration issue at this period was very poor, and had to be constantly supplemented out of Regimental funds. Mrs. Chisholm also donated a very acceptable supply of necessaries and provided still another occasion for the grateful thanks of Australian soldiers in Egypt.

Cricket now began to assist in passing away the spare hours. With a good deal of difficulty a mud and matting wicket was provided and troop and squadron matches finally culminated in a victory over the Wellington Regiment, and the despatching of a Regimental team to Cairo.

Towards the end of April Captain Mackenzie, who had been Adjutant to the Regiment since June, 1917, left for embarkation to Australia on special 1914 leave. Receiving his commission on Gallipoli, he steadily established his reputation as a troop leader, and during the Sinai and Palestine campaigns his efficient conducting of screen work became the feature of many a night ride into enemy country. In this respect his work during the dash on Bir Salmana was particularly noteworthy.

The country towards Salmana on the route
taken by the Regiment was quite unknown. The
night was particularly unfavourable, but Lieut.
Mackenzie's work with map, compass and star
brought the column to the exact point laid down
in the operation orders at the exact time, a feat
which was probably unequalled in the history of
the Regiment's night marches. His work as Adjutant bore the same marks of his unassuming
efficiency, and all ranks, no less than his brother
officers, said good-bye to "Mac" with genuine
regret. His place as Adjutant was taken by Lieut.
N. C. Nevitt.

The month of May found the Regiment still at
Quesna. All chance of our speedy departure
seemed to be receding further from us as the weeks
went by. Duties went on as usual. Occasional
patrols, town pickets, and ordinary Regimental
duties varied slightly the monotony of camp life.

During May the Fellaheen were paid for grain
and forage requisitioned at different periods of
the war, and it became a daily job for an officer
and section to accompany Egyptian pay officials to
different villages in the district. The hospitality
shown by the village Omdahs on these occasions
took the form of a prodigious lunch to the soldiers,
and this glimpse into the life and customs of rural
Egypt provided at least one interesting feature of
our post-war "campaign."

Early in May Lieuts. Ross and Reynolds left
on leave for the United Kingdom, Lieut. Gurney
reported back from detached duty in Cairo, and

Lieut. MacGillivray was absorbed from the Divisional Train.

Towards the end of May everyone was heartened by the definite news of an early move to Kantara to await embarkation. This finally eventuated on the 1st and 2nd of June. The Regiment arrived at Kantara in two batches, and after immediately handing in all horses to the Remount Depot, less a few transport and officers' chargers, proceeded to Mrs. Chisholm's canteen, where a meal had been provided.

The new (and last) camp was stationed a mile across the Canal. Ample tent accommodation was available; duties were few, and sports were well catered for by cricket grounds and tennis courts. A cinema and beer canteen, in addition to the delights of the salt water, helped to pass the last lap with a minimum of discontent among the men.

The cricket competition finally closed leaving the 7th Regiment the winner but the final match between them and the 6th was drawn, after a very strenuous game. The batting of Artie Reynolds and "Trig" Farguhar, against the bowling of Hooker and Middleton, was worthy of a first-grade contest, and both bowlers showed an equally high pitch of excellence.

The month crept slowly away. We even knew now the name of our transport. Rifles, saddlery, and all gear had been handed in and it seemed impossible to slip this time. Nevertheless we *did* slip a day after tents had been struck and handed

in, and the desert emphasized its tinge in our sys-
tems as we lay for the last time on the red sand
and under the scanty shade of a bivvy sheet.

But it all ended at last.   On the 28th of June
we cleaned up a camp for the final time, and made
our way independently to the Canal.   The *Madras*
came in sight from Port Said about 2 p.m.   The
whole of the Brigade, with the exception of the
Field Ambulance, embarked in quick time, and by
6 o'clock we were moving slowly southward.

Two days which we had often despaired of ever
seeing arrived in one.   Often we had wondered
how we would feel when they arrived; most of
us, by now, had become impervious to any real
thrills, and our embarkation for home and the
signing of peace left the majority of men to all
appearances less moved than by the one-time prospect of a week's leave to Cairo.

The strength of the Regiment as it embarked
was 15 officers and 391 other ranks.   Major D.
G. Cross, who had temporarily commanded the
Regiment since Lt.-Col. Fuller took charge of the
Brigade, remained our O.C., and achieved the
rather unique record of being the only officer in the
Regiment who left with it and returned with it.
But compared with his record and reputation in
the field, such an achievement is of only casual im-
portance.   Probably the Regiment never possessed
another squadron leader with the all-round attain-
ments of "Roarer" Cross.   In every department
of military work, in a peace camp, on points of
training, in placing an outpost line, or in actual

Major D. G. Cross, who commanded the Regiment from
December, 1918, to August, 1919.

action, Major Cross was essentially both sound and brilliant, and as second in command during the Beersheba operations, his able assistance to his C.O. (Temp. Lt.-Col. H. D. White) went far towards the success of the Regimental share in the big drive from Beersheba to Jaffa. That such an officer should return undecorated, after nearly five years active service will ever remain one of the Regimental anomalies, and an illustration of subtle unfairness somewhere.

The disposition of the remainder of the officers on the journey home was as follows:

Headquarters—Major S. A. Tooth, D.S.O., 2nd in Command; Lieut. N. C. Nevitt, Adjutant; Captain Hanton, Quartermaster; Lieut. Gurney, Pay Duties; Educational Officer, Lieut. E. H. Moll.

A Squadron—Captain Menzies, Captain N. Dickson and Lieut. Lowe.

B. Squadron—Captain H. Dickson, M.C., Lieuts. Campbell and Berrie.

C Squadron—Major Close and Lieuts. Evans and Macansh, D.C.M.

With the exception of Major Cross, every returning officer left Australia in the ranks, and all but four in the original regiment. Of the rank and file, one original man, Driver J. P. McCormack returned with it.

The homeward voyage of the *Madras* was not particularly noteworthy. The weather through the Red Sea and for several days after passing Aden was intensely hot. All the deck accommodation, with the exception of portion of the starboard saloon deck, was available for other ranks, and occupied by them day and night.   The sea was, generally speaking, moderate throughout. A few boisterous days were experienced between Aden and Colombo.   Sports and concerts were arranged, and a full day's excursion to Kandy gave nearly half the personnel of the Regiment the experience of the tropical scenery and natural beauties of Ceylon.   But everything faded into insignificance beside the one outstanding fact: every turn of the screw was bringing us closer home.

Medical regulations prevented shore leave at Fremantle, and an inspection resulted in some 50 men from the Brigade being landed and placed in quarantine. We stayed in Fremantle Harbour 24 hours, and then, with Melbourne as our next stop, rounded the Leeuwin and entered the rolling waters of the Bight.   The monotony of the remainder of the voyage was broken only by a few hours shore leave at Melbourne, and on the 3rd of August the Regiment arrived home.

Sixth Light Horse Regiment
Casualties—Gallipoli

KILLED IN ACTION

32	Tpr. Murray, V.		Capt. W. Lang
188	Sgt. Parkes, S.	643	Tpr. Dalzell, D. P.
646	Tpr. Jeffrey, N. S.	594	Tpr. McCay, D. R.
375	Tpr. Brown, H. S.		Lieut. A. F. Buskin
	Lieut. H. Robson,		Capt. R. Richardson
452	Tpr. Ronald, K. M.	153	Tpr. Matthews, F. W.
508	L/Sgt. Ellis, F.	184	Tpr. Young, J. H.
443	Tpr. O'Brien, W. H.	725	Tpr. Ingram, W. B.
495	Tpr. Kidman, W.	882	Tpr. O'Neill, L. H.
195	Sgt. Tresillian, F.	520	Tpr. Stevens, E. B.
255	Tpr. Flanagan, C.	1095	Tpr. Lawrence, J. W.
502	Tpr. Stewart, F.		

DIED OF WOUNDS

748	Tpr. Pattrick, E.	39	Tpr. Gatenby, G. L.
726	Tpr. Bonnar, W.	787	Tpr. Harris, W. J.
231	Tpr. Bellinger, P. J.	828	Tpr. Wilson, R.
392	L/Cpl. Creer, E. J.	139	Tpr. Halloran, C. R.
122	Tpr. Gibson, M. R.	857	Tpr. Carter, J. O.
411	Tpr. Farrar, A. F.	1112	Tpr. Raynor, W. T.
361	Sgt. Lamborne, G.	877	Tpr. Manion, F.
291	Tpr. Morris, G.	300	Cpl. McDonald, J. W.
809	Tpr. O'Dell, S.		

DIED OF ILLNESS

710	Tpr. Dunn, G.		Capt. A. Verge
169	Tpr. Robertson, W.	571	Tpr. Bacon, C.

WOUNDED

	Lieut.-Col. Cox	102	Tpr. Chisholm, H. B.
595	Tpr. Strickland, S.	933	Tpr. Cornish, H. J.
391	L/Cpl. Cornish, W.	125	Tpr. Gibbons, H. A.
184	Tpr. Young, J. H.	266	Tpr. Gurner, N. C.
374	Tpr. Bergelin, R. W.	139	Tpr. Halloran, C. R.
494	L/Cpl. Hudson, S.	723	Tpr. Hill, C. E.
	Capt. M. F. Bruxner	141	Tpr. Jaques, L. W.

	Lieut. A. R. Hordern	286	Tpr. Marsden, H. F.
748	Tpr. Pattrick, E. V.	807	Tpr. Naesmith, J.
536	Tpr. Almond, P.	655	Tpr. Penrose, W.
39	Tpr. Gatenby, G. L.		Capt. W. Lang
274	Tpr. Isted, F. J.	819	Tpr. Rathbone, A. R.
668	Tpr. Young, W.	706	Tpr. Spinney, R. W.
114	Tpr. Fryer, D.	325	Tpr. Woods, J.
638	Tpr. Casey, J.	331	Tpr. Walker, C. J.
207	Cpl. Cheater, J. H.	477	Tpr. Warby, W.
183	Tpr. Yeomans, G. H.	560	Tpr. Wilson, H.
43	Sgt. Moffatt, H.	629	Tpr. Whitby, J. W.
351	Tpr. Woods, F. M.	826	Tpr. Wiggins, W. H.
863	Tpr. Drady, H. R.	828	Tpr. Wilson, R. 2nd
500	Tpr. Sherwin, C. R.		Occasion
88	Cpl. Baldie, D. W.	80	Tpr. Burgess, W. R.
58	Cpl. Quintal, F. E.	87	Tpr. Brown, W. H.
738	Tpr. Hill, F.	627	Tpr. Booker, C. E.
567	Tpr. Culley, J. S.	488	Tpr. Cousins, W. M.
213	Tpr. Stevens, H. E.	489	Tpr. Cornet, F. S.
827	Tpr. Woods, J. T.	666	Tpr. Crockett, T. E.
122	Tpr. Gibson, M. R.	248	Tpr. Dally, S. M.
828	Tpr. Wilson, R.	250	Tpr. Elliott, W. A.
323	Tpr. Tindall, S.	260	Tpr. Fender, W. M.
791	Tpr. Kinnane, W.	509	Tpr. Frizell, F. G.
726	Tpr. Bonnar, W.	649	Tpr. Foote, W. J.
329	Tpr. Waters, G. R.	568	Tpr. Holloway, B. L.
339	Sgt. Collins, E. R.	439	Tpr. Morton, E.
361	Cpl. Lamborne, G.	506	Tpr. O'Neill, W. J.
231	Tpr. Bellinger, P. J.	305	L/Cpl. Pickering, H.
526	Tpr. Thompson, J. R.		G.
535	Tpr. Allen, A.	818	Tpr. Rowling, H. G.
94	Tpr. Carne, A. N.	883	Tpr. Rose, E.
319	Tpr. Sherwin, N. D.	370	Tpr. Gill, C. R. D.
138	Tpr. Hole, J. F.	731	Tpr. McKenzie, W. M.
720	Tpr. Miller, W.	414	Tpr. Gee, A.
178	Tpr. Vernon, G.		Lieut. D. Drummond
299	Tpr. McEwan, W.	117	Tpr. Gurney, A. B.
522	Tpr. Scott. C. S.	206	Tpr. Watts, H. W.
453	L/Cpl. Ronald, R. B.	280	Tpr. Lawson, O.
669	Tpr. Wrigley, L.	388	Tpr. Callaway, B. F.
152	Tpr. Muffett, R. F.	399	Tpr. Collins, F. J.
287	Tpr. McMahon. S.	553	Tpr. Blake. G. E.
590	Tpr. Weston, R. H.	892	Tpr. Snowden, F.
337	Sgt. Menzies. S. M.	640	Tpr. Mulholland, E.
107	Tpr. Ewin. F.	799	Tpr. Morris. W. J.
293	Tpr. McDougall. H. E.	800	Tpr. Maloney, J. R.
820	Tpr. Ray. A.	819	Tpr. Rathbone. A. R.
47	Sgt. Smith, S.		2nd Occasion

629	Tpr. Whitty, J. W.	857	Tpr. Carter, J. O.
79	L/Cpl. Blackmore,	888	Tpr. St. Leger, A. R.
	L. G.	715	Tpr. Bloomfield, J. R.
610	Tpr. Body, G. C.	854	Tpr. Brennan, J. T.
612	Tpr. Body, T. C.	87	Tpr. Brown, W. H.
518	Tpr. Capel, C. R.	1001	Tpr. Arundale, A.
519	Tpr. Capel, K. C.	1112	Tpr. Raynor, W. T.
566	Tpr. Chauncey, E. L.	877	Tpr. Manion, F.
792	Tpr. Daly, R. A.	981	Tpr. Smith, F.
411	Tpr. Farrar, A. F.	1016	Tpr. Foley, J.
422	Tpr. Humpheries, H.	1106	Tpr. Plackett, T. W.
	E.	551	Tpr. Brazel, P.
361	L/Sgt. Lamborne, G.	966	Tpr. Smith, D. A.
	2nd Occasion	300	Cpl. McDonald, J. W.
291	Tpr. Morris, G.	278	T/Cpl. Kelly, H. J.
878	Tpr. Mulroney, N.	531	T/Cpl. Waygood, A.
44	Tpr. McKeown, G. R.		E.
615	Tpr. McCarthy, H.	962	Tpr. Smith, L. F.
441	Tpr. Norden, C.	1118	Tpr. Waters, E.
809	Tpr. Odell, S.	926	Sgt. Doyle, P. J.
448	Tpr. Paul, C. S.	193	Sgt. Fisher, A.
31	Tpr. Reed, E. T.	1084	Tpr. Dwyer, J. J.
168	Tpr. Robinson, A. N.	1078	Tpr. Broadfoot, W. S.
451	Tpr. Rodd, R. J.	939	Tpr. Digby, N.
735	Tpr. Reid, A. S.	1064	Tpr. Booth, N. J.
213	Tpr. Stevens, H. E.	399	Tpr. Collins, F. J.
	2nd Occasion		2nd Occasion
743	Tpr. Walker, O. B.		

Casualties—Sinai and Palestine

KILLED IN ACTION

	Capt. N. M. Pearce ..	..	..	..	29/7/16
2241	Tpr. Wilson, H. N. ..	..	..	..	4/8/16
219	Tpr. Ritchie, J.	..	..	..	4/8/16
930	Tpr. Crozier, R. W. ..	..	..	..	4/8/16
1489	Tpr. Kelleher, J.	..	..	..	4/8/16
1049	Tpr. Wright, E. A. M.	..	..	..	4/8/16
780	Tpr. Davis, D.	..	..	..	4/8/16
836	Tpr. Drady, H. R. ..	..	..	..	5/8/16
1526	Tpr. Ussher, L. A. F.	..	..	..	17/4/17
	Capt. A. C. Thompson	..	..	..	2/11/17
1416	Tpr. Warren, G. H. ..	..	..	..	3/11/17
1108	Tpr. Prendergast, A. J.	..	..	..	3/11/17
229	Sgt. Barrow, F. G. ..	..	..	..	8/11/17
1210	Tpr. Bloodworth, R. J.	..	..	..	29/11/17

R 2

1065	Tpr. Christie, H. J.	29/11/17
	Lieut. O. W. Tooth	3/12/17
588	Tpr. Barton, B. T.	3/12/17
1121	Cpl. White, F. A. F.	27/3/18
1209	Tpr. Hawkey, R. J.	27/3/18
740	Sgt. Loveband, L. W.	27/3/18
399	L/Cpl. Collins, F. J.	27/3/18
2420	Tpr. Riley, K. C.	27/3/18
1322	Tpr. Makeig, W. C.	27/3/18
2869	Tpr. Boyle, E.	28/3/18
1058	Tpr. Galbraith, F. R.	28/3/18
3539	Tpr. Presland, T.	25/9/18
1932	Tpr. Pryor, L. A.	28/3/18
1487	Tpr. Johnston, L. J.	28/3/18
2330	Tpr. Gallaher, L. N.	28/3/18
232	Sgt. Burlace, W. H.	28/3/18
	Lieut. F. L. Ridgway	28/3/18
2377	Sgt. Sharpe, W. L.	28/3/18
1642	Tpr. Maybury, R. C.	28/3/18
1692	Tpr. Wilkins, C.	28/3/18
531	Tpr. Waygood, A. E.	28/3/18
226	Tpr. Bradshaw, A.	28/3/18

DIED OF WOUNDS

639	Sgt. Johnson, M.	18/8/16
939	Tpr. Digby, N.	6/8/16
	Lieut. R. Black	17/8/17
410	Sgt. Foster, R. J. (M.M.)	6/11/17
306	Sgt. Potter, W. W.	3/12/17
1492	Tpr. Kniepp, N.	19/12/17
825	Tpr. Vance, T. H.	27/3/18
3534	Tpr. Gear, G. C.	29/3/18
2942	Tpr. Baker, E. J.	29/3/18
1425	Tpr. O'Brien, A. J.	29/3/18
343	Tpr. Tebbutt, H. V.	20/9/18
1492a	Tpr. Donnisson, G. F.	29/3/18
319	Tpr. Sherwin, N. D.	29/3/18
759	Tpr. Crozier, S. J.	29/3/18

DIED OF DISEASE

1376	Tpr. Anderson, H. H.	4/2/17
1203	Tpr. Maslen, J. A.	8/10/17
2935	Tpr. Sholefield, G. D.	23/12/17
86	Tpr. Bult, A.	15/2/18
2333a	Tpr. Gummow, C. G. J.	11/8/18
412	Tpr. Gill, G. R.	19/9/18
3021	Tpr. Johnson, N. M.	16/10/18

3306	Tpr. Petersen, A. O.	..	..	..	28/10/18
3711	Tpr. Chase, L. J.	..	..	..	..	11/11/18
875	Tpr. McCarthy, R. C.	..	..	..	23/2/19

REPATRIATED PRISONERS OF WAR

1386	Tpr. Gannon, F. A.
948	L/Cpl. Hewitson, A. R.
2382	Tpr. Spencer, C. L.
2346	Tpr. Lambert, L.
3048	Tpr. Clarke, R.
257	Tpr. Farley, H. C.
619	Sgt. King, W. J.
1233	Tpr. MacPherson, J. D.
1129	L/Cpl. Moll, W.
858	Tpr. Crockett, A.

DIED OF DISEASE WHILE PRISONERS OF WAR

3027	Tpr. Smith, C.
1111	Cpl. Redman, C. T.

DIED AFTER RETURNING TO AUSTRALIA

Sgt. R. Thorne
Q.M.S. J. Cheater
Sgt. R. Strachan
Cpl. J. Brady

WOUNDED

459	Tpr. Smith, R. R. B.	..	..	..	28/7/16
399	Tpr. Collins, F. J. ..	..	3rd Occas.	28/7/16
	Lieut.-Col. C. D. Fuller (D.S.O.)	..	6/8/16
1558	Tpr. Johnson, W.	..	..	..	20/7/16
318	Tpr. Semmens, H. ..	..	..	..	4/8/16
1568	Tpr. Siddons, A. J. R.	..	..	..	5/8/16
208	Cpl. Suffolk, J. W. ..	..	..	..	4/8/16
1448	Tpr. Bright, J. H. R.	..	..	..	4/8/16
1174	Tpr. Meares, C. L. D.	..	..	..	4/8/16
454	Tpr. Rock, W. F. ..	..	..	..	5/8/16
1184	Tpr. Rogers, F. E. ..	..	..	..	4/8/16
339	Sgt. Collins, E. A. ..	..	..	..	4/8/16
705	Tpr. Carter, A. J. ..	..	..	..	4/8/16
199	Tpr. Keast, R. M. ..	..	..	..	4/8/16
1701	Tpr. Stratford, S. W.	..	..	..	4/8/16
1151	Tpr. Arnott, F. ..	..	..	..	4/8/16
500	Tpr. Sherwin, C. R. ..	..	..	..	4/8/16
1476	Tpr. Hargreaves, J. ..	..	..	..	4/8/16
1354	Tpr. Suttor, P. L. ..	..	..	..	4/8/16
1543	Tpr. Fraser, P. ..	..	..	..	4/8/16
55	Tpr. Perry, T. F. ..	..	..	..	4/8/16

702	Cpl. Boorman, H. J.		4/8/16
1173	Tpr. May, R. ..		4/8/16
1087	Tpr. Frogley, O. R.		4/8/16
354	S.M. Weir, W. J. A.		4/8/16
448	Cpl. Paul, C. S.		4/8/16
1156	Tpr. Dowling, N. R.		4/8/16
470	Tpr. Sweeney, C.		4/8/16
1548	Tpr. Hayes, S. G.		4/8/16
2232	Tpr. Saunders, J. M.		4/8/16
381	Tpr. Burns, W.		4/8/16
1044	Tpr. Shoemark, C. R.		4/8/16
2204	Tpr. Murphy, H. C.		4/8/16
564	Sgt. Collins, H. G.		5/8/16
1301	Tpr. Anderson, C. P.		5/8/16
1276	Tpr. O'Sullivan, D. M.		5/8/16
1197	Tpr. Wilson, P. A.		5/8/16
814	Tpr. Price, W. H.		5/8/16
1421	Tpr. Williams, E. A.		5/8/16
28	Tpr. Little, P. C.		5/8/16
2885	Tpr. Mountain, W. C.		5/8/16
1108	Tpr. Prendergast, A. J.		5/8/16
410	Sgt. Foster, R. J. (M.M.)		5/8/16
928	Tpr. Brown, W. H.		5/8/16
499	Tpr. McCullogh, D.		5/8/16
402	L/Cpl. Deveson, E.		5/8/16
159	Tpr. McDonald, H. T.		10/8/16
1055	Tpr. Rohrick, J. H.		12/8/16
746	Cpl. Ridgway, F. L.	Accidentally	15/8/16
250	Tpr. Elliott, W. A.		17/4/17
258	Tpr. Fisk, S. N.		19/4/17
442	Tpr. Nash, G. B.		19/4/17
1572	Tpr. Wallace, G. A.		19/4/17
1093	Tpr. Kerchert, D. A.		20/4/17
1778	Tpr. Harmer, W. H.		8/7/17
965	Tpr. Shearer, J.		8/7/17
335	R.S.M. Hanton, J.	Accidentally Injd.	19/7/17
2655	Tpr. Porritt, J. N.		19/7/17
1490	Tpr. Kennewell, G. F.		19/7/17
	Lieut. R. Black (M.C.)		16/8/17
	Lieut. H. Dickson (M.C.)		2/11/17
208	Cpl. Suffolk, J. W.		3/11/17
1417	Tpr. Warren, R. W.		3/11/17
1259	Tpr. Day, C. H.		3/11/17
307	Cpl. Strachan, R.		31/10/17
2868	Tpr. Beacom, W. H.		9/11/17
	Lieut. H. Dickson (M.C.)	2nd Occas.	10/11/17
1708	Tpr. Lavender, V. M.		8/11/17
2423	Tpr. Danvers, J. F.		10/11/17

1030	Tpr. McNamee, O. H.	..	..	..	10/11/17
233	Sgt. Burlace, W. H. ..	..	..	..	10/11/17
702	Sgt. Boorman, H. J. 2nd Occ., Rem on duty				
					10/11/17
1050	Tpr. Webster, C.	..	..	..	8/11/17
3243	Tpr. Hodge, J.	Rem. on duty			10/11/17
2322	Tpr. Eldershaw, E. ..	..	..	..	19/11/17
1686	Tpr. Watt, E.	..	..	..	22/11/17
	Lieut. R. B. Ronald ..	..	..	..	29/11/17
1064	Tpr. Booth, W. J. ..	..	..	..	29/11/17
115	Tpr. Farrell, T.	..	..	..	29/11/17
1326	Tpr. McCormack, T. F.	..	..	..	29/11/17
3231	Tpr. Best, R. ..	..	..	..	29/11/17
2484	Tpr. Heckenberg, J.	Rem. on duty			29/11/17
527	Sgt. Baird, D. M.	..	..	..	3/12/17
	Lieut. N. Dickson	..	..	..	3/12/17
377	Sgt. Bargh, J. M. ..	..	..	..	3/12/17
812	Sgt. Reynolds, N. S.	..	..	..	3/12/17
1114	Cpl. Saunders. H. G.	..	..	..	3/12/17
2990	Tpr. Chitty, T.	..	..	..	3/12/17
2461	Tpr. Dill, C. D.	..	..	..	3/12/17
2333	Tpr. Holdsworth, N.	..	..	..	3/12/17
1310	Tpr. Lowe, H. D. G.	..	..	..	3/12/17
721a	Tpr. McMicking. Q. G.	..	..	..	3/12/17
2366	Tpr. O'Keefe, T. ..	..	..	..	3/12/17
1104	Tpr. Perry, W.	..	..	..	3/12/17
1575	Tpr. Winter, M. H. J.	..	..	..	3/12/17
1324	Tpr. Meldrum, G. ..	..	..	..	3/12/17
469	Cpl. Smith, C.	..	..	..	3/12/17
517	Cpl. Busby, E. A.	Rem. on duty			3/12/17
571	Tpr. Ausburn, H. J.	Rem. on duty			3/12/17
794	Tpr. Kerwick, N. P.	..	..	..	3/12/17
518	Cpl. Capel, C. R.	..	..	..	3/12/17
2952	Tpr. Allen, E. B. ..	..	..	..	3/12/17
569	Tpr. Stibbard, D. C.	..	..	..	3/12/17
434	Tpr. Minahan, M. ..	..	..	..	3/12/17
85	Tpr. Bush, G. E.	..	..	..	10/12/17
1208	Tpr. West, A. S.	..	..	..	27/3/18
1447	Tpr. Brind, S. E.	..	..	..	27/3/18
3648	Tpr. Barton, D. H. ..	..	..	..	27/3/18
3673	Tpr. Snell, J. T.	..	..	..	27/3/18
3238	Tpr. Gleeson, W. J. ..	..	..	..	27/3/18
1132	L/Cpl. Ekin, W. H.	..	..	..	27/3/18
1053	L/Cpl. Yates, C. B. ..	..	..	..	27/3/18
2232	Tpr. Saunders, J. M.	..	2nd Occas.		27/3/18
866	Cpl. Gillham, C. H. ..	..	..	..	27/3/18
1768	L/Cpl. Warden, A. M.	..	..	..	27/3/18

2260	Tpr. Johnston, W. G.	.. .. ..	27/3/18
2400	Tpr. Weate, K. D. ..	.. .. ..	27/3/18
1687	Tpr. Weir, G. A. ..	.. .. ..	27/3/18
1464	Tpr. Dunbar, A.	.. .. ..	27/3/18
	Lieut. G. V. Evans ..	.. .. ..	27/3/18
2224	Tpr. Scurrah, G. L. ..	.. .. ..	27/3/18
961	Tpr. Schmierer, A. S.	.. ..	27/3/18
307	Tpr. Strachan, R. F.	Rem. on duty	27/3/18
3369	Tpr. Rathbone, A. R.	.. .. ..	28/3/18
1180	Tpr. Newlands, E. S.	.. .. ..	28/3/18
232	Tpr. Burbank, E. ..	.. .. ..	28/3/18
3351	Tpr. Colgan, T. D. ..	.. .. ..	28/3/18
461	Tpr. Stougie, S. ..	.. .. ..	28/3/18
744	Tpr. Fitzgerald, T. ..	.. .. ..	28/3/18
3236	Tpr. Finlayson, S. B.	.. ..	28/3/18
2307	Tpr. Bassett, W. P. (M.M.)	.. ..	28/3/18
1130	Cpl. Cochrane, A. ..	.. .. ..	28/3/18
1207	Cpl. McCann, W. ..	.. .. ..	28/3/18
1288	Tpr. Ferris, A. G. ..	.. .. ..	28/3/18
	T/Major H. S. Ryrie	.. .. ..	28/3/18
3058	Tpr. Lockwood, B. A.	.. .. ..	28/3/18
1402	Tpr. Orr, L.	.. .. ..	28/3/18
1608	Tpr. Davis, H. W. ..	.. .. ..	28/3/18
2988	Tpr. Beach, W.	.. .. ..	28/3/18
5261a	Tpr. Pierce, F. T. ..	.. .. ..	28/3/18
1189	Tpr. Smith, R. ..	.. .. ..	28/3/18
	Lieut. A. B. Campbell	.. .. ..	28/3/18
1763	Tpr. Latimore, A. J.	.. .. ..	28/3/18
2148	Tpr. Barnes, E. ..	.. .. ..	28/3/18
	Lieut. H. G. Lomax ..	.. .. ..	28/3/18
	Major D. G. Cross ..	.. .. ..	28/3/18
1347	Tpr. Williams, A. T.	.. .. ..	28/3/18
649	Tpr. Foote, W. J. ..	.. .. ..	28/3/18
	Lieut. H. Dickson (M.C.) Rem. on duty, 3rd Occas.		28/3/18
1010	Tpr. Bell, J.	Rem. on duty	28/3/18
1346	Tpr. Webb, B. ..	.. .. ..	29/3/18
3349	Tpr. Blake, G. C. ..	.. .. ..	31/3/19
541	Cpl. Single, S. ..	.. .. ..	1/4/19
1156	Cpl. Dowling, N. R. Accid. Inj. in Action		27/3/18
3302	Tpr. McAlister, W.	Shell Shock	28/3/18
3363	Tpr. Lloyd, J. R. ..	.. .. ..	13/4/18
191	Sgt. Brown, R. ..	.. .. ..	19/4/18
801	Tpr. Mayes, E. C. ..	.. .. ..	19/4/18
1465	Tpr. Farley, B. ..	.. .. ..	19/4/18
3675	Tpr. West, J. C. D. ..	.. .. ..	3/5/18
1571	Tpr. Thoroughgood, R.	.. .. ..	30/4/18

2018	Tpr.	Chinnock, A. E.	..	..	..	30/4/18
1482	Tpr.	Hindmarsh, S. R.	..	..	..	4/4/18
5358	Tpr.	Greentree, J.	Self	Inflicted		20/6/18
3300	Tpr.	McMahon, E. ..	..	..	..	16/7/18
2237	Tpr.	Taylor, W. J. ..	..	..	..	16/7/18
1052a	Tpr.	Lea, J. W.	Rem.	on	duty	16/7/18
1538	Tpr.	Donaldson, J. H.	..	..	..	25/9/18
2426	Tpr.	Saunders, C. W.	..	..	..	25/9/18
2658	Tpr.	Richards, R. F. T.	..	..	..	25/9/18
2617	Tpr.	Whiles, J. L. ..	..	..	..	15/9/18

W. C. Penfold & Co. Ltd , 83 Pitt Street, Sydney.

www.ingramcontent.com/pod-product-compliance
Lightning Source LLC
Chambersburg PA
CBHW031946080426
42735CB00007B/286